PRAISE FOR
WHO SPEAKS FOR GOD?

"This is more than a book. It is a manifesto that sends a clarion call to Christians who want to unite in creating a new kind of compassionate politics in America."
—Tony Campolo, professor of sociology,
Eastern College

"Jim Wallis is in a league of his own when it comes to his ideas on forging a new spiritual politics that speaks to all Americans."
—Dean Smith, head basketball coach,
University of North Carolina

"WHO SPEAKS FOR GOD? provides a valuable reflection on the spirit in which people of faith must go about discerning in the light of the gospel the challenges and opportunities which presently face us."
—Walter F. Sullivan, bishop of Richmond, Va.

"Jim Wallis's WHO SPEAKS FOR GOD? is at once a penetrating critique of the religious right and a most thoughtful exploration of the proper role of religion in public life. Anyone who cares about these issues—and we all should—must read this book."
—Rabbi David Saperstein

"THE MOST IMPORTANT POLITICAL BOOK YOU CAN READ." —*Values & Visions*

'WHO SPEAKS FOR GOD?

An Alternative to the Religious Right—A New Politics of Compassion, Community, and Civility

Jim Wallis

Delta
Trade Paperbacks

A Delta Book
Published by
Dell Publishing
a division of
Bantam Doubleday Dell Publishing Group, Inc.
1540 Broadway
New York, New York 10036

ISBN 0-385-31693-3

Reprinted by arrangement with Delacorte Press

Manufactured in the United States of America
Published simultaneously in Canada

December 1997

10   9   8   7   6   5   4   3   2   1

BVG

This book is dedicated to my friends and colleagues in the Call to Renewal—Tony Campolo, Marie Dennis, Wes Granberg-Michaelson, Eugene Rivers, Ron Sider, and the many others who are offering a new spiritual politics beyond the old categories of Left and Right, liberal and conservative.

Contents

Acknowledgments

The writing of any book involves not only an author, but an extended community. Ideas and inspirations come both through interaction and in solitude. When a book is connected to a sense of movement, as this one is, the community dimension is even stronger. This book arises out of a deepening hunger among many to find a "third way," a more "spiritual politics" beyond the old polarized options of Left and Right, liberal and conservative. It connects to a new national network named the "Call to Renewal" seeking both to offer an alternative to the Religious Right and to help forge a new politics in America.

So I begin by thanking my close colleagues in the Call to Renewal steering committee—Tony Campolo, Marie Dennis, Wes Granberg-Michaelson, Eugene Rivers, and Ron Sider. Add to them the hundreds of other religious leaders who have already joined together. Our launching statement, "The Cry for Renewal," is reprinted in the appendix.

I also want to thank my co-workers at *Sojourners* magazine, which for many years has tried to make the connections between "faith, politics, and culture," and whose editorial staff discussions provide a regular context for discussion of all three. I also want to thank the members of the Sojourners Community Church and the staff of Sojourners Neighborhood Center in the inner city of Washington, D.C., who are seeking every day to live out a new vision of spiritual politics.

I especially want to thank my longtime friend and editor Roy M. Carlisle, whose steadfast encouragement and skilled editorial assistance has helped me birth another book. Thanks also go to Steve Ross, my fine editor at Delacorte, and Gail Ross, my able and enthusiastic agent, both of whom believed in this book and made it happen. I am grateful also to People for the American Way, whose careful monitoring of the Religious Right has provided many facts and quotations from its organizations and leaders.

Special thanks go to Joy Carroll for her constant support and inspiration during the writing.

Introduction

The topic of politics and religion is in the air, and it has been for some time now. Everybody is talking about it—from *Reader's Digest* to *Rolling Stone*. The central concern today is the "values crisis," or what Senator Sam Nunn described as a "deficit of the soul" at the 1996 National Prayer Breakfast. Whether they are religious or not, most Americans are hungry for a deeper connection between politics and moral values, many would say "spiritual values."

But for too long, the so-called Religious Right has dominated that discussion in the mainstream media. The result is that many people who have religious and spiritual concerns, but don't feel represented by groups like the Christian Coalition, feel left out of the conversation. I want to see those people brought back into the public discussion. We need them.

We live in the most religious country in the world. Many Americans across the liberal-moderate-conservative political spectrum are deeply religious or "spiritual" people. They, too, believe that their country is losing its way morally, they, too, see a vital connection between values and politics, they, too, if they are religious, believe the language of faith *is* relevant to political life. But if they don't warm to the polemics of television preachers who sound like right-wing ideologues, where are they to turn? I want those people to find somewhere else to go.

But our problem is not just a "Christian Coalition" which claims to speak for all religious people. It is also the mostly liberal secularists who want to keep *any* religious or spiritual concerns out of politics altogether. Their antireligious bias is as rigid and intolerant as the Christian fundamentalists on the other side. These have become our false choices: hollow secularism or right-wing religion. Many people are hungry for an alternative; the good news is that there is one. I want to suggest another way.

A few clarifications. First, the "Religious Right" should not be made into a category into which all social conservatives are dumped. Thoughtful conservatives in America are making valuable contributions to our discourse about morality and "virtue" in the public square, the sacred value of human life, the problems of bureaucracy in government, the need for taking personal community responsibility, et cetera. Conservatives are not all part of the Religious Right, even religious conservatives.

Second, all those Americans who are attracted to the Religious Right should not be lumped in with every political position of groups like the Christian Coalition. Many are drawn to the Religious Right out of concern for the decline of values in their country, fear for their children's future, moral conviction about the nation's abortion rates, or reaction to what they see on their television sets no matter what time of the day they turn them on. It's a mistake to believe everyone who is part of the Religious Right wants to take over the country and impose a repressive theocratic regime on their neighbors.

But some of the Religious Right's leaders *are* extreme and their agenda bodes danger for the country. Since they are now actively competing for political power (and getting it), their views and agenda should be made known and they should be held politically accountable for them. Because their claim is also religious, as well as political, the Religious Right should also be scrutinized by religious and specifically biblical criteria. I want to help us attempt that task together.

Many of the references and quotations I've used refer to the Christian Coalition, and its president, Pat Robertson. That is because the Coalition is the largest, best mobilized, and most powerful Religious Right organization in the country and indeed has become one of the most powerful groups in the nation.

Despite the fact that many people, including many conservatives, think Robertson's views are quite bizarre, the political power his Christian Coalition has amassed makes those views no longer fringe. It makes them important, and the subject of needed public attention, especially from the religious community.

The Religious Right is moving and changing just like the rest of us. In the past year, some of their leaders and organizations have begun to express a new concern for the plight of poor people in America and the sin of racism. Though these are new issues on their agenda, I don't believe they should simply be written off as politically insincere or merely opportunistic, as some of their critics have done. My conversations with both leaders and followers in the Religious Right have persuaded me that some of them are now genuinely convinced of the biblical imperative for such social conscience. Where that will lead politically, no one can tell.

Already, very interesting schisms are appearing between religious conservatives and the much more libertarian corporate elites in the Republican party over issues such as the impact of corporate downsizing on families, the privatization of Social Security, and U.S. policy toward human rights violations and religious persecution in China. There was already tension between the two groups over issues such as pornography, abortion, and the values of music, movies, and television produced by corporations that are more profit-minded than family-centered. Could a new economic populism be emerging among some quarters of the Religious Right? Again, only time will tell, but some truly unexpected conversations are now occurring between very diverse Christian leaders at roundtables set up to find common strategies for confronting poverty.

Indeed, this book is much less about Pat Robertson and the Christian Coalition than it is about a "new politics"—a politics with spiritual values that transcends the old categories of Left and Right, liberal and conservative.

The vital question in religion and politics today is, indeed, "Who speaks for God?" I've tried to provide some help in answering that question and in seeking to forge a more spiritual politics. When I think of "spiritual politics," I often think of Mohandas K. Gandhi. The spiritual and political leader of India's freedom struggle warned against what he called "The seven deadly sins." They were: "politics without principle, wealth without work, commerce without morality, pleasure without conscience, education without character, science without humanity, and worship without sacrifice." Clearly, Gandhi's maxims speak to the heart of our moral crisis today. The issues he raises are much deeper than the battles between the Democrats and the Republicans. Wherever I travel, the reciting of Gandhi's warnings elicits a deep response in people across the political spectrum. Perhaps it's because the West has made Gandhi's "deadly sins" into a way of life—and we are now paying the price.

Together, we must search for a spiritual politics suited to our own time, a politics of compassion, community, and civility. Ultimately, we are searching for a new politics of hope.

WHO SPEAKS
FOR
GOD?

ONE

Who Speaks for God?

"The Constitution of the United States says nothing about the separation of church and state. That phrase does appear, however, in the Soviet Constitution, which says the state shall be separate from the church and the church from the school. People in the educational establishment have attempted to impose Soviet structures on the United States."
—Pat Robertson, *Conservative Digest*

"The Constitution of the United States, for instance, is a marvelous document for self-government by Christian people. But the minute you turn the document into the hands of non-Christians and atheistic people they can use it to destroy the very foundation of our society."
—Pat Robertson, *The 700 Club*

The Religious Right is right when it says we have a spiritual crisis in America. But the answer to a spiritual crisis is something far deeper than electing as many right-wing Republicans to office as possible, as the Christian Coalition is trying to do. That's where the Religious Right goes wrong.

Most people, religious or not, sense that something is wrong in America. The polls say most of us believe the nation is fundamentally "off track." Things seem to be unraveling and coming apart. The values and bonds that hold life, families, and communities together feel like they are collapsing.

Our streets are not safe. Too many marriages are not working, too many children are not being loved and protected, too many families are falling apart. Too many politicians are not trusted, too many corporations value profits above all else, too many schools are not educating, too many people are falling between the cracks, and too many kids are getting left behind. There is too much violence, cheapened sexuality, and false materialistic values in our movies and on our television sets.

In both the personal and public spheres of life, promises are not being kept. Our commitments are not being honored, our responsibilities not being taken seriously. The economic gaps between us are growing, racial polarization is on the rise, and threats to our natural environment hover over us like a storm cloud. The sacred value of human life seems no longer to be a value at all.

Because of these things, most Americans are very worried about the future of their children. And that is not a good sign for the health of any society.

The Religious Right has tapped into the public longing for a new focus on "values" and the need for "spiritual renewal." Most of the liberal Left hasn't figured that out yet, even though most Americans have. But the Religious Right goes wrong in thinking a crisis of spiritual values can be solved by resorting to partisan political warfare. The solutions must go beyond ideological politics and the power games between Republicans and Democrats. Their Christian Coalition has merely become a "power bloc" in the Republican party.

But the political conclusions reached by the so-called Christian Right are not very convincing to a lot of other people, *including* a lot of other Christians. While the media reinforces the impression that all Christians who care about politics are right-wingers, many other Christians think the Religious Right is wrong—about a lot of things.

A spiritual crisis demands a "spiritual politics." But neither the Religious Right nor the secular Left have yet to grasp what that might mean. The good news is that there is a third alternative—one that has the power to transform our political landscape by getting to the moral heart of the issues at stake and empowering those who are moved by matters of the spirit but left dry by today's divisive public debate.

Voting "Christian"

Some television preachers want to tell you not only how to vote, but how to vote "Christian." Their "Christian Coalition" tries to dictate who the "real" Christian candidates are; the funny thing is, they're almost all right-wing Republicans.

Although they are called the "Religious Right," they don't talk much about Jesus at all, or about the Hebrew prophets; nor do they discuss the kind of spiritual values that might bring us together, or heal the nation's wounds, or uplift the poor, as you might expect from a group that proclaims itself the voice of religion in politics. Instead, they tell us who to be afraid of.

In the spring of 1995 Christian Coalition founder and president Pat Robertson wrote a series of letters to members of Congress telling them that to support the Republican welfare bill and tax cuts for the rich was the Christian thing to do. Consequences for not voting "Christian" on these bills were implied.

Executive Director Ralph Reed may run the day-to-day operations of the Christian Coalition, but Pat Robertson hired Reed and is still his boss. Robertson, the television preacher and millionaire broadcaster of *The 700 Club,* is still clearly the controlling force behind the Christian Coalition's powerful political machine with 1.7 million members, a budget of $25 million, the boasted control of the Republican party apparatus in already half of the states, and the most clout of any single power bloc in the GOP. That's what makes his extreme theological and political views so dangerous and important.

Representative Glenn Poshard is a fourth-term Democratic congressman from a poor rural district in Illinois. He is also a devout Southern Baptist layman and former church deacon who seldom misses his weekly prayer meeting with other members of Congress who are fellow believers. But Congressman Poshard thought the Republican welfare proposals were too harsh on poor women and children. The Bible teaches us to defend the rights of the weak and vulnerable, said the Illinois lawmaker on the floor of the House of Representatives, not to strip away their meager resources while, at the same time, giving the biggest tax breaks to our wealthiest citizens. Rarely had a congressional speech given on the House floor contained as many biblical references as Representative Poshard's.

As a Christian and a conservative on certain issues, Representative Poshard shares some positions with the Christian Coalition, but not this time. He began his speech in the House by saying, "With all due respect to the Christian Coalition, where does it say in the Scriptures that the character of God is to give more to those who have and less to those who have not? . . . If there is one thing evident in the Scriptures, it is that God gives priority to the poor." The congressman went on to demonstrate that point by quoting several passages of Scripture, including the words of Jesus from the twenty-fifth chapter of Matthew's gospel, "I was hungry, and you gave me food. . . . As you have done it to the least of these, you have done it to me."

The next day Representative Poshard got a phone call from the Christian Coalition. As Christians addressing a fellow believer, what they should have said was something like: "Brother Glenn, we disagree with your biblical interpretation. And we would like to sit down with you and have an honest discussion between Christians about the issues at stake here." But instead, the Christian Coalition was incredulous that Poshard would disagree with their position. The Coalition lobbyist was quite upset. In the 1996 elections, Glenn Poshard was targeted by the Republican party.

I am an evangelical Christian. But I am deeply disturbed by what *evangelical Christian* connotes in American public life today. A divisively strident, massively mobilized, and politically powerful new movement has burst upon the political scene, putting forward a highly partisan and ideological agenda—in the name of God.

In God's Name?

Who *does* speak for God? It's a good question, and a very old one, as kings, presidents, generals, popes, preachers, and prophets of every stripe have enlisted the name of God to bless and support their various causes and schemes. Today, in American politics, the name of God is invoked by the Religious Right to support such specific political platforms as the abolition of the Department of Education, the defunding of National Public Radio, or the repeal of the Endangered Species Act.

Sometimes in history the name of God has been invoked on behalf of actions and movements that have ennobled the human soul and lifted the body politic to a higher plane. Take the Reverend Martin Luther King, Jr., and the American civil rights movement, or Archbishop Desmond Tutu and the struggle against South African apartheid, as examples. Other times religious fervor has been employed for the worst kinds of sectarian and violent purposes. The Ku Klux Klan, the troubles in Northern Ireland, the wars in the former Yugoslavia, and David Koresh's Branch Davidian standoff in Waco, Texas, are frightening examples.

Is there a reliable guide to when we are really hearing the voice of God, or just a self-interested or even quite ungodly voice in the language of heaven? I think there is. Who speaks for God? *When the voice of God is invoked on behalf of those who have no voice, it is time to listen. But when the name of God is used to benefit the interests of those who are speaking, it is time to be very careful.*

In his epistle to the little church at Corinth, the apostle Paul writes, "But God chose what is foolish in the world to shame the wise; God chose what is weak in the world to shame the strong; God chose what is low and despised in the world, things that are not, to reduce to nothing things that are, so that no one might boast in the presence of God."

Well, there is quite a lot of "boasting in the presence of God" in American politics today. At the Christian Coalition's "Road to Victory" Conference in 1995, a political and cultural "holy war" was proclaimed in the name of God with all the major Republican presidential candidates invited to speak and court the cheering Christians. But such religious confidence in God's political purposes generally has little to do with the "weak, lowly, and despised."

Virtually every religiously based social movement of great historical significance has been *on behalf of others.* Slaves, women, children, oppressed peoples, racial minorities, exploited workers, political prisoners, refugees, disenfranchised populations, persecuted believers, and victims of war have all been the subjects of religiously and morally inspired social movements.

On the other hand, the religiosity of movements that merely advance the economic and political interests of their own constituencies is far more suspect. Religion has been used in the self-defense of slaveholders, dictators, conquering warriors, captains of industry, security police, and the rulers of both church and state.

The crucial difference is who benefits from the voice of God being spoken and heard. Indeed, answering that question helps to tell us if we are really hearing the voice of God at all, or just the self-interest of the religious voices.

Who speaks for God today? The Religious Right would have us believe that it does. And the media has been very cooperative, giving right-wing fundamentalists most of the coverage when the issues of politics and religion come up. And these days religion and politics come up all the time.

For several years now the loud voices of the Religious Right have virtually controlled the national discussion of politics and morality with the help of the media, who have consistently ignored alternative voices. And with all its money the Religious Right has literally been able to buy its own microphones and broadcast its political message into every American household and to millions more around the world.

Taking a Poll

Imagine yourself standing on any street corner in America today, whether it's the street on which you live, or downtown, or next to a college campus—any street from Miami to Seattle. Picture the first ten people you meet—a cross section of ages, ethnicities, and incomes—and ask them the same question: "What do the words *evangelical Christian* mean to you?" Chances are that, despite the range of backgrounds and experiences they carry with them, most of their answers will be the same.

The most likely answers you will hear are "Religious Right" or "right-wing," "fundamentalist," and invariably "conservative Republican." In the minds of many the word *evangelical* has now become almost totally identified with a particular and very partisan political stance. Evangelical Christianity has come to represent a very potent political force and the most important power bloc within the Republican party.

For more than a year I've been asking very diverse audiences of people around the country that very thing—what would they hear on the street corners of their own city in response to the question "What is an evangelical Christian?" or even, "What is a Christian?" On literally every occasion the words I always hear back are the conservative right-wing labels. Names of the most famous Religious Right groups or people are often cited—"The Christian Coalition," "Pat Robertson," or "Jerry Falwell." When pressed about the political views of such Christians, a whole series of "antis" is quite predictable: not only "antiabortion," but also "antiliberal," "antifeminist," "antigay," "anti–secular humanist," "antiwelfare," "anti–affirmative action," "antiimmigration," "antienvironmentalist," "antihomeless," "antiurban," and "antipoor." (The Religious Right thinks wealth is a sign of God's favor, and by implication people are poor due to their own moral failings—they call it the "prosperity gospel" and it bears about as much resemblance to the message of Jesus as the TV preachers' fund-raising methods do to His Sermon on the Mount about trusting God to take care of us like the lilies of the field.)

Most Christians believe abortion *is* a moral issue, and most Americans are troubled by enormously high abortion rates in their country. In such a chaotic and dangerous environment as America today there are plenty of things worth being against, and any approach to politics must offer real solutions to our many problems. But on the Religious Right, politics seems to be *defined* more by what people are afraid of, and who they think is to blame for the nation's ills.

Judging by their words and deeds the activists of the Christian Right aren't exclusively "anti." But what they seem to be most strongly "for" are politicians who promise to "take back the country, precinct by precinct," generals who believe America's military firepower is God's arsenal against evil in the world, businessmen who have made a fortune, television preachers who have made a fortune, and men who believe that they should take over again as the heads of their households.

If you ask the average American about how the zealots of Religious Right usually express their political views, you're likely to hear back: "harsh," "divisive," "self-righteous," "intolerant," or "mean spirited." Indeed, the Religious Right offers their political views in the name of God, and by implication those with contrary opinions are considered outside the will of God, or "not really Christian." Which doesn't make other Christians feel very good at all.

These public perceptions of the Religious Right are remarkably consistent whether the questions are being asked in Pennsylvania, Colorado, Mississippi, New York, or California. The Religious Right has become such a strong and singular media voice on matters of politics and morality that the word *Christian* is now synonymous with their particular brand of very conservative Republican politics. When television anchors like Dan Rather discuss the role of "Christian activists" in various political campaigns, they always mean the Christian Right.

For those of us who are both Christian and actively engaged in public issues but are *not* right wing, this is an alarming development. Recently, in England, a young evangelical youth worker asked me a very worried question. "Is it true now in America that when someone is converted to Christ, they are automatically associated with the Christian Coalition whether they want to be or not?" In her country evangelical Christians who try to apply their biblical perspectives to political issues may come out on the Left, Right, or Center, depending upon the question at hand. She feared that the ideological predictability of the American Religious Right would give

Christianity a bad name. Indeed. The truth is that America's Christian Right is an extreme and unique phenomenon not found anywhere else in the Western world.

But the Christian Right does not represent all the Christians in America, or even most of them. The media-created perception of a right-wing evangelical juggernaut is the most tragic *misperception* in American politics today. It is time to change that perception.

Let's first take another poll on that street corner. Ask those same passersby what they think Jesus was like. Almost universally, whether those being questioned are themselves religious or not, you will hear things like "compassionate," "loving," "caring," "humble," "friend of the poor and outcasts," "forgiving of sinners," "critic of the establishment," "nonviolent peacemaker," "reconciler," a different kind of king whose kingdom is meant to break down the walls people have put up between themselves. How do we explain the contradictions here? Either the popular picture of Jesus is mistaken or Pat Robertson's Christian Coalition has the wrong political agenda.

Reclaiming a Tradition

Evangelical used to be a good word, one with connotations many would admire. It means a biblically rooted and Jesus-centered faith, and it comes from the word *evangel*—which means "good news." Jesus himself used the word to announce the meaning of His coming. There, standing in the temple in the little town of Nazareth, he quoted Isaiah's ancient prophecy, "The Spirit of the Lord is upon me, because he has anointed me to preach good news [the evangel] to the poor. . . ."

But the Religious Right preaches a message that is more ideological than truly evangelical and includes little about Jesus at all. Their political preference for wealth, power, and military might flies in the face of a gospel that was intended to be good news to the poor and was preached by an itinerant Jewish rabbi who said that it was the peacemakers who would be blessed.

It is very important to remember how today's Religious Right began. One issue, more than any other, sparked the movement that is today such a powerful force in American politics. That issue is the million and a half abortions in America each year since the historic Supreme Court decision of *Roe* v. *Wade* in 1973. Concern for the unborn first galvanized religious conservatives. Political liberals and the whole left side of the American political spectrum saw no moral issue at stake except a "woman's right to choose." Only recently have a few voices in the pro-choice movement admitted that there is more than one life (the mother's) involved in the moral equation of abortion. We will deal with the issue of abortion later in this book, and attempt to find some common ground between warring political factions. But the point here is that the initial impulse of what has become the Religious Right *was* a passionate moral concern for "the other."

However, the Religious Right's pro-life stance has become morally *inconsistent*. Their advocacy for human life seems to extend only from conception to birth. It is a profound tragedy how a movement founded in legitimate concern for the unborn transformed itself into one that fights *against* equal rights for women, civil rights for homosexuals, public policies to aid the poor and redress racial injustice, regulations for environmental protection, school lunches and virtually every federal program for children. It is painful to see how that organized concern for life has developed into a group that fights *for* more nuclear weapons and handguns, expanding the death penalty and the numbers of people in prison, increasing tax breaks for the rich while decreasing welfare for the poor, and creating a nation that most benefits people who are white, middle class, suburban, and Christian.

By contrast the American Catholic bishops, who are also against abortion, have adopted a very different political stance called "a consistent ethic of life." It's a religious commitment to defend human life and values like a "seamless garment" wherever and whenever they are threatened—by abortion, euthanasia, poverty, racism, capital punishment, nuclear war, or the violation of human rights. It's an independent political posture that cuts across the traditional categories of Right and Left.

One wonders whether the Religious Right even knows its church history. In the last century evangelical Christians were leaders in the abolitionist movement against slavery, were tireless advocates of the poor and oppressed, and were in the forefront of the struggle for women's rights! But today's Religious Right agenda is hardly good news to the poor, women, and disadvantaged racial communities.

The tenets of today's Religious Right stand in sharp contrast to the prophetic tradition of America's religious history. Both Quakers and evangelical revivalists led the abolitionist movement against slavery. Charles Finney, the leading evangelist of the nineteenth century and the Billy Graham of his day, directly equated revivalism with abolitionism. He is said to have invented the altar call in order to sign up new converts for the antislavery cause. Like their English counterparts John and Charles Wesley, Lord Shaftsbury, and William Wilberforce, American revivalists were also outspoken on behalf of workers, children, public education, and prison reform. And until this century most of the movements for women's suffrage and equality had religious roots.

In this century Dorothy Day and her Catholic Worker movement were an early precursor for Catholic social teaching, which now emphasizes the "preferential option for the poor." Martin Luther King, Jr., and the black Baptist preachers of the civil rights movement held their Bibles in one hand and their Constitutions in the other, as they took their fight for freedom to the streets and into prison cells throughout the South, even while the Bible-belt predecessors of the Religious Right opposed them. Abraham Joshua Heschel showed that the Jewish vision of "shalom" demanded an end to racial and economic injustice as he marched alongside Dr. King. Daniel and Philip Berrigan demonstrated how Christian peacemaking often requires active resistance to the policies and practices of war. In the 1980s churches provided the animating core of the antinuclear movement, opened themselves up as "sanctuaries" for Central American refugees fleeing tyranny, and were blamed by the U.S. State Department for halting U.S. funding for the Contra War in Nicaragua. In 1990 Nelson Mandela came to the U.S. to thank American church leaders for their leadership in applying successful American economic sanctions to the white South African regime. Virtually all of these efforts were opposed by those who today constitute the Religious Right.

It is important to recognize what a historical aberration the Religious Right represents. For biblical religion to be put at the service of the rich instead of the poor, the powerful instead of the oppressed, of war instead of peace, turns Christian teachings upside down. For evangelical religion to be used to fuel the engines of racial and class division, to block the progress of women, to undermine care for the creation, to fight the banning of assault weapons, to end public legal services to those who can't afford them, and actually encourage a public policy that abandons our poorest children runs counter to Christian Scripture, tradition, and history. The Religious Right has accomplished an almost complete reversal of Christian teaching and all in the name of God. What happened?

The Hijacking

Here's what happened. A big split in American Protestantism at the turn of the century left the churches divided in the early 1900s between "fundamentalists" and "modernists." The two sides polarized over issues like the relationship between science and religion and the authority of the Bible. There was also a tragic schism between personal conversion and social justice, with the conservatives withdrawing from "worldly concerns" and the liberals neglecting the need for spiritual transformation. But after the Second World War a new evangelical movement began to emerge. It sought to reintegrate evangelical faith with both intellectual inquiry and social concern. By the early 1970s a group of younger evangelical pastors, professors, and seminarians were pressing hard for social justice to be high on the evangelical agenda.

The Chicago Declaration, issued in 1973, expressed

that rising evangelical social conscience over such fundamental issues as poverty, racism, sexism, and war. Widely respected evangelist Billy Graham, evangelical senior statesmen like England's John R. W. Stott, and mainstream evangelical colleges and publications also demonstrated "the social implications of the gospel," perhaps best expressed in the Lausanne Covenant of 1974. It appeared that the evangelical social responsibility of nineteenth-century revivalists was about to be rediscovered.

But suddenly, seemingly out of nowhere, the American evangelical movement was "hijacked," according to evangelical scholar Tom Sine. By the early 1980s new groups like the Moral Majority had begun to steer the evangelical parade in a different direction. Evangelical Christianity was quickly commandeered by a combination of television preachers and right-wing political operatives who met together in non–smoke-filled rooms and recognized their common cause and the power to be gained by taking over the evangelical label. Veteran conservative political activists met with fundamentalist preachers to strike a bargain for political power. Using genuine evangelical concerns like rising abortion rates and the cultural breakdown of moral values, the political Right's computers were aimed at lists of evangelical constituents supplied by the television preachers, and the mobilization of evangelical voters for a comprehensive right-wing political agenda had begun.

Claiming religious discrimination, the new Religious Right demanded coverage from the media and got it. Combined with their own powerful TV shows and radio stations, their reach extended quickly across the nation. An often alarmist media response only made the power of the television preacher/politicians look even more formidable. Some liberal reporters seemed to think if the religious fundamentalists were given enough rope they would hang themselves. Instead, the media-savvy preachers and activists of the Religious Right effectively used the media for their own purposes. Not since the civil rights movement had the American media been used so successfully to promote a cause. The Religious Right has by now become so successful that the nation today perceives the discussion of religion and politics to be almost their exclusive domain. The media, having little understanding of religion, focused mostly on the growing political influence of the Religious Right and paid no attention to whether the right-wing evangelical activists bore any resemblance to the historic Christian tradition.

For example, in the debate over much-needed welfare reform, the Christian Coalition supports cutting support to single mothers and their children, despite the fact that these women and children are modern-day equivalents of the "widows and orphans" for whom the New Testament shows such special concern. At the same time the Religious Right strongly supports lowering taxes for wealthy families and cutting the capital gains tax, which everyone knows would most benefit the richest people in the country. Now, that is a kind of economic redistribution, but hardly the kind that the biblical writers had in mind.

In the biblical concept of the Jubilee Year, for example, land was to be periodically returned, debts forgiven, and prisoners released. The purpose of this regular "redistribution" was to bridge the gaps between rich and poor by evening things out at least a little. By contrast, in the Christian Coalition's concept of sound public policy, the rich would accumulate even more land and money, the poor would lose welfare and be dumped into an economy with too few jobs that can support a family, and more prisons would be built to lock up the criminals. (It's more than ironic that the Religious Right, which so vehemently opposes the theory of evolution, has come to embrace social Darwinism's idea of the survival of the fittest.)

Likewise, the Christian Coalition and its conservative Republican allies use race as a wedge issue in the affirmative action debate instead of seeing continued racism in America as a spiritual and theological offense demanding repentance. In fact, lack of leadership on the issue of race is perhaps the greatest moral failure of the Religious Right and their conservative political bedfellows. The absence of black faces, voices, and concerns throughout the programs and pronouncements of the

Religious Right is a glaring deficiency. Black Christian leaders have testified to being "out of the loop" of the Christian Coalition and their agenda. The alienation is now so deep that Pentecostal minister Reverend Eugene Rivers referred to the Coalition, in a recent *USA Today* article, as the "Afrikaner wing of the fundamentalist flat-earth coalition."

Who Represents Christians?

The majority of American Christians, and even most evangelical Christians, do not belong to the Religious Right. To resurrect an old term, what might be called the Silent Majority of Christians are definitely not in lockstep with the vocal Christian Coalition. The editors of *Christianity Today,* the foremost evangelical publication in the country, estimate that only one third of America's evangelicals are with the Religious Right, another third are more moderate or progressive in their politics, and another third are unsure what political stance to take. Most Catholics would take their political leads from their bishops and the pope rather than from the Christian Coalition. While theologically and culturally conservative, the nation's twenty-five million black Christians have an entirely different social and political agenda than Religious Right Republicans. And the vast majority of the country's mainline Protestants are looking for a biblically based social concern instead of an ideologically rooted partisan religion on the Right or the Left. Those millions of "other Christians" cannot be dismissed with labels like "liberal" or "secular human-ist," as the Religious Right always characterizes those who disagree with them.

Most American Christians do not challenge the Reli-gious Right's "right" to bring its religious values into the public square as some political liberals have. On the contrary, we believe the impoverished political process needs the moral direction and energy that spiritual and religious values can contribute to the public debate. The rightful separation of church and state does not and must not prohibit the positive influence of religious val-ues on the nation's political climate. Morality is vital to politics, and more and more Americans are feeling the urgent need to connect the two.

The question is not *whether* religious faith should make a political contribution, but *how*. If religious val-ues are to influence the public arena, they ought to make our political discourse more honest, moral, civil, and spiritually sensitive, especially to those without the voice and power to be fairly represented. That is where the Religious Right has failed most profoundly. Since the 1980s the powerful influence of the Religious Right has helped make our political debate even more divisive, polarized, and less sensitive to the poor and dispos-sessed.

When Christian Coalition Executive Director Ralph

Reed announced in early 1995 that his allegedly non-partisan organization would spend $1 million to spread the Republicans' Contract With America throughout the churches, it signified that the Religious Right's union of evangelical religion with partisan politics was now complete.

On May 18, after the Christian Coalition released its own Contract with the American Family, National Public Radio's Alex Chadwick asked Ralph Reed what the Christian Coalition hoped to accomplish over the next five to ten years. Reed replied, "What we aspire to be is a permanent fixture on the American political landscape for people of faith, just as the Chamber of Commerce is for business, or just as the AFL-CIO is for union workers, or just as the Veterans of Foreign Wars are for veterans."

Then Reed defined what he meant by "people of faith" as "those with devout faith, those who have sought to elevate a sense of civility and a sense of values in our society, those who attend church or synagogue and who testify to a religious commitment." Now, that's a pretty big group. It represents most people I know. Reed says he desires to give us all a "voice in government." The problem is that many people who fall into Mr. Reed's definition of "people of faith" don't want to be politically represented by the Christian Coalition or the Religious Right. Their voice is *not* our voice.

The Need for an Alternative Voice

While the press has focused on the strident voices of the Religious Right, a more prophetic and inclusive movement for spiritual and social change has been steadily growing. This quieter movement includes not only evangelicals but many Catholics; black, Latino, Asian, and Native American Christians; mainline Protestants; Jews; Muslims; and those with no religious affiliation but a spiritual hunger.

Many of us care deeply about moral values, the breakdown of family life, and the erosion of personal responsibility in our neighborhoods and nation. But that doesn't lead us into the arms of the Religious Right. On the contrary. We believe that social responsibility is at the heart of our biblical traditions, that racism and sexism are sins, and that the best test of a nation's righteousness is not its gross national product and military firepower but, according to the prophets, how it treats the poorest and most vulnerable. We seek to recover moral virtue, to renew family life, to rebuild our communities, and to forge new bonds of healing and reconciliation across the social and cultural chasms that still divide us.

Above all, we want to forge a politics of *vision* that will not engage in endless and divisive recrimination, but could infuse the political process with a new sense of hope. What is at stake is not just politics, but the meaning of faith itself. Aggressive right-wing litmus tests have distorted the independent moral conscience that faith can bring to politics. The integrity of religious conviction has been slandered by a narrow ideological agenda. Authentic religion has been subverted when wealth and power are extolled instead of being held accountable; and when the gospel message is turned upside down to bring more comfort to those on the top of society than to those at the bottom.

The Religious Right has claimed an exclusive right to define evangelical faith by its own political agenda. Because the word *evangelical* has become so identified with a particular political and cultural militancy, many evangelical Christians now hesitate to identify themselves as such. But the term *evangelical* should not be abandoned, it must be reclaimed.

A Call to Renewal

The night before the National Prayer Breakfast in early February of 1995, a group of evangelical leaders met in Washington, D.C., to discuss the serious problem of the Religious Right's ascendancy, and the need for an alternative voice. Ever since the 1994 fall elections a new conversation had been taking place among evangelicals and was quickly spreading to other church constituencies. All agreed, the time had come to challenge the Religious Right and offer a deeper perspective—a clear, visible, and public alternative that lifted up another vision of the relationship between faith and politics.

Today evangelical voices across the country are seeking a biblical approach to politics, away from the ideological agenda being advanced by the Religious Right. Alongside them are Catholic voices that affirm their church's social teachings as a clear alternative to both Religious Right and secular Left. Black, Latino, Asian, and Native American Christian voices have no trouble combining family values with a commitment to social justice; and they have never entirely embraced either liberal or conservative politics. A new chorus of voices throughout the Protestant churches is seeking to transcend both old religious liberalism and the Christian Right's fundamentalism. Jewish voices are calling us back to the Hebrew prophets who focus our attention on the downtrodden and the peaceful vision of "shalom."

From these many voices new networks representing alternatives to the Religious Right began to form. In the spring of 1995 more than a hundred Christian leaders from a diversity of traditions joined in issuing a call entitled "The Cry for Renewal." It sent a clear message to the nation's media and political leaders: "Let other voices be heard."

The statement began, "Our times cry out for renewed political vision. And vision depends upon spiritual values. We believe that the language of morality and faith

can make a critical contribution to political discourse.
. . . But if politics will be renewed more by moral values than by partisan warfare, the religious community must play a more positive role. . . . Christian faith must not become another casualty of the culture wars. Indeed, religious communities should be the ones calling for a cease-fire."

History teaches us that ideological conformity tends to corrupt political convictions that are based on religious faith. The "Christian militias" in Michigan and Montana proof-text the Bible to shore up their extremist agenda on the Right, just as Jim Jones led his People's Temple followers to death in Guyana with revolutionary religious appeals from the Left. Even in more mainstream movements we have seen far too much religious conformity on both sides of the political spectrum. For much too long conservative evangelicals have been the Republican party at prayer, and liberal religious leaders have been too easily confused with the left wing of the Democratic party.

"The Cry for Renewal" challenged both sides. "The almost total identification of the Religious Right with the new Republican majority in Washington is a dangerous liaison of religion with political power. With the ascendancy and influence of the Christian Right in party circles, the religious critique of power has been replaced with the religious competition for power." The signers of the statement also critiqued "the continuing close identification of religious liberalism with political liberalism and the Democratic party," and said that "moral imagination" and "prophetic integrity" must become more important than the pursuit of political access and influence.

The heart of "The Cry for Renewal" was a call for a new morally based politics that transcends the old categories of Left and Right. "We refuse the false choices between personal responsibility or social justice, between good values or good jobs, between strong families or strong neighborhoods, between sexual morality or civil rights for homosexuals, between the sacredness of life or the rights of women, between fighting cultural corrosion or battling racism. We call ourselves and our churches back to a biblical focus that transcends the Left and the Right. We call the Christian community to carefully consider each social and political issue, diligently apply the values of faith, and be willing to break out of traditional political categories. By seeking the biblical virtues of justice *and* righteousness, the Christian community could help a cynical public find new political ground." Therein lies the hope.

"The Cry for Renewal" called for a new dialogue with *all* sectors of the religious community. But it clearly said the Religious Right had dominated long enough. They have one perspective and deserve to be heard. But the issues of political morality are too important to be left only to one voice. Other visions of faith and politics exist in the land and must now be lifted up. "Our commitment is to diligently apply spiritual values to the vexing questions of our public life and, where necessary, to offer a Christian alternative to ideological religion."

Challenging the Powers That Be

On Tuesday, May 23, 1995, five days after Ralph Reed, on NPR, said the Christian Coalition aspired to be a "permanent fixture" representing "people of faith," a delegation representing a broad group of Christian leaders gathered in Washington, D.C., to make a statement to the press and meet with the political leadership of both the Democratic and Republican parties. The group was led by evangelical Christian leaders to correct the media-created public impression of a monolithic right-wing evangelical tidal wave. There was a strong and complementary unity in the different voices, and together the message was made very clear.

Many who spoke have been doing the things we testified to long before the Religious Right grabbed the nation's microphones. Ron Sider, of Evangelicals for Social Action, was there, who has worked tirelessly to promote social concern in the evangelical community. So was Tony Campolo, the popular evangelist who believes people are converted to Christ in order to make a difference in this world, and not just to prepare for the next one. Presidents Roberta Hestenes of Eastern College and Steve Hayner of the international student organization InterVarsity Christian Fellowship, represented the concerns of a new generation of evangelical leaders, while the new general secretary of the Reformed Church in America, Wes Granberg-Michaelson, showed how a new breed of mainline Protestant leaders is anxious to build bridges across old dividing lines.

James Forbes, senior pastor of the Riverside Church in New York City, brought the poetic and Pentecostal power of the black churches, while Eugene Rivers and Ray Hammond from Boston's Ten Point Coalition carried that authentic message from the streets. Margaret Cafferty, executive director of the Leadership Conference of Women Religious, voiced the conviction of eighty thousand Catholic sisters who teach the children, run the soup kitchens, and bind up the wounds of those who suffer from callous public policies. And Jim Dunn of the Baptist Joint Committee explained in his slow Southern drawl why he "gets irritated" when right-wing Christians claim to speak for born-again Texas Baptists like himself.

It was a great day and the phone hasn't stopped ringing since. The press coverage was extensive and fair, from the national newspapers to the hometown dailies across the country. It was clear that a need had been recognized and a responsive chord had been struck.

The meetings our delegation had with both Republi-

can and Democratic political leaders proved to be much
more substantive than we had expected. We told them
that religious conviction must not be manipulated for
partisan purposes, and that we sought an honest dialogue with all political leaders about holding the process
more accountable to moral values.

We pushed Speaker of the House Newt Gingrich and
House Majority Leader Dick Armey on their lack of
alternative strategies and resources for local communities in the face of massive proposed Republican social
cuts at the federal level. We pressed House Minority
Leader Dick Gephardt and his Democratic congressional colleagues on the need for a new approach at the
community level beyond just defending the current welfare state. And we had very good discussions with legislators like then Senator Bill Bradley about the need to
reinvigorate the "civil society" with new public-private
partnerships for solving social problems. The hunger
and need for a new political conversation beyond liberal
and conservative, Left and Right, was apparent in all of
our meetings.

On May 23 we raised up a clear, public, and visible
alternative voice to the Religious Right. Other voices
from the religious community were finally being heard.
We brought together a new network of spiritual and
social concern across the life of the churches, with the
widest coalition that people have seen for many years.
"The Cry for Renewal" united conservative evangelicals

and Pentecostals, black church leaders, Catholic bishops and women religious, and the heads of most of the Protestant churches. As Wes Granberg-Michaelson said at the press conference, "This is a real Christian coalition."

Spiritual Crisis

Nine months later, after the 1996 National Prayer Breakfast, 250 local pastors and church-based activists came to Washington from every region of the country. Their purpose: to mobilize and organize a grassroots alternative to the Religious Right and lift up a new political vision that speaks to the nation's deep spiritual crisis. Out of their early-February working conference in 1996 they said, "The soul of our nation hungers for prophecy and thirsts for vision." From every corner of the nation they testified that while conservative Christians have tapped into people's genuine longing for a new emphasis on values in public life, that longing is for alternatives much wider and deeper than the narrow interpretations offered by the Christian Coalition.

New options are necessary, they said, and a moral vacuum is waiting to be filled. People in our communities are searching for another way. An evangelical church elder in Michigan told me that "the Religious Right is trying to saw a two-by-four with a hammer. People know that something needs to be fixed, but are searching for the right tools to fix it. Right now the Christian Right claims to have the only tools. But more and more of us aren't sure that they really do."

What *are* our deepest and best values? And if we are indeed in the midst of a *values crisis,* what is the best response? To elect as many right-wing Republicans to office is hardly an adequate response to a spiritual crisis. Yet, that is the only program the Christian Coalition has. It has no other evident agenda.

If the crisis we now face in this country, and in the West, is indeed one of the spirit, it calls for more than politics as usual and, for that matter, religion as usual. The old political categories of liberal and conservative, Left and Right, are completely dysfunctional now, and helpless to lead us into a better future. The spiritual crisis we must confront pleads for nothing less than what the biblical tradition calls "the healing of the nation." The prophetic biblical vision always combined justice and righteousness, social transformation and moral integrity. We desperately need such a vision today.

I saw a graffito on the side of a wall recently that summed up our spiritual wasteland quite well: *Work. Consume. Be silent. And die.* Does the materialistic right-wing agenda of the Religious Right even begin to address the depth of that despair? The Christian Coalition has shown that they are not spiritual enough for the job. Most all of the social and political issues we are facing have a moral core, and real social change will not take place without a change in our moral values as well.

What we must learn from the mistakes of the Christian Right is that religious concern cannot be simply identified with a partisan agenda. Not only is it dangerous, but the solutions of partisan ideological politics will simply not be adequate. Therefore, the alternative to the Religious Right is not the Religious Left. That is still a mistake that many who oppose the Religious Right are making. It's time to transcend the old ideological polarities that control our public life. We need something deeper. We need a new and different kind of politics—a politics whose values are more spiritual than ideological.

For years now the Religious Right has dominated the public debate on politics and morality, suggesting that the only alternatives are either to be completely secular or to subscribe to their right-wing politics. That dominance may be coming to an end.

New Politics

Upon his retirement from public office Senator Bill Bradley honestly lamented his own lack of courage as a legislator. Instead of following his heart and conscience, he now believes he too often went along with the process and the system, which mostly ignore the underlying moral and spiritual issues at stake in politics today.

When asked what those issues were by one interviewer, Bradley named five key areas: our relationship to the land and the environment; honestly coming to terms with our own history—good and bad; seeing our racial and ethnic diversity as a strength rather than a weakness; confronting the problem of a changing global economy and its threats to both the poor and the middle class; and encouraging each individual to explore his or her spiritual nature and values. That's a much deeper and wider view of the relationship between morality and politics than we normally hear from the Religious Right, and a deeply encouraging one. More and more political leaders are now searching for a deeper kind of politics, but many of them are retiring from public office. At the same time many are looking, like so many other Americans, for a better way to effect the direction of public life in the United States.

Religious values can help us find the path to a new politics. The spiritual politics that we need must be rooted in the values of *compassion, community,* and *civility*. These three can be viewed, in fact, as religious *tests* of politics. And they will be the subjects of the rest of this book.

Compassion is the first test of politics, from a religious perspective. A new politics of compassion would especially focus on those whom Jesus called "the least of these." It is a selective morality indeed that ignores the Bible's deep concerns about economic justice and racial reconciliation in a divided society. From the Religious Right we simply don't hear that cry being raised with the power of Jesus or of Amos, who called upon his hearers to "let justice roll down like waters and righteousness like a flowing stream."

How do we treat the poor, the stranger, the outcast, the weak, the vulnerable, the children? The Hebrew prophets saw this as the truest criterion of a nation's integrity. With this measure of compassion as a moral beacon, we can move beyond the old categories of Left and Right as we make our way through the questions of social policy and welfare reform toward the alleviation of poverty. We must transcend the tired debates between defending old welfare bureaucracies or balancing the budget on the backs of our poorest children. Neither maintaining poverty nor abandoning the poor is a moral option.

The second test of politics is community—whether our political policies and processes build or destroy our common life. Martin Luther King once wrote that the choice before us was "chaos or community." Because we have rejected the latter we are now faced with the former. The breakdown of family and community in our nation must focus our attention on reweaving the fabric of life and relationships that has so seriously eroded. The gangs and violence that now plague even our middle-size and small towns are a direct consequence of the breakdown of family, community, and economy. They all must be repaired.

A renewed sense of community at both local and national levels would aim at bridging our racial, economic, and social divides; and a politics of hope might offer the vision that both liberals and conservatives have failed to provide. Many people are already engaged across the country in grassroots efforts to fashion a new political community. Their stories and experience must become a part of the national discussion.

Our third test of politics is civility—the character of our public discourse and decision making, and the participation of ordinary people in the political process. The politics of warring factions, "us and them" rhetoric, and the polemics of fear and blame, must be seriously critiqued from a religious perspective. In particular the religious community must challenge the Right to stop blaming the poor, the urban underclass, the homeless, the blacks, the homosexuals, and the feminists. And the liberals must be challenged to stop stereotyping and caricaturing evangelicals, conservatives, and religious commitment generally, or belittling "traditional," "moral," and "family" values.

We must try to find common ground by moving to higher ground on a whole range of issues, including some of the most incendiary issues like abortion and homosexuality. Could we not recognize both the sanctity of human life and the equality of women? Couldn't we strongly support the rebuilding of traditional two-parent families while we stop scapegoating homosexuals as if they are responsible for the breakdown of our families?

Many today feel the need for a third path of politics between the diatribes of the Right and the Left. We reject the extremes on either end of the political spectrum that now control and poison our political life, while actually preventing us from reaching solutions. We envision a "moral center" ("radical middle," *Newsweek* has called it) for politics, and contend that a refocusing on "values" and even our "religious values" can help us get there.

The problems this nation faces do indeed call for a change of heart. It is the spiritual transformation of our values that is most required. All the truly great social movements had such a spiritual transformation at their core. We need the strength and involvement of the religious community more than ever—but not only one voice, and not just a partisan voice. The political witness we need today from the religious community will be more prophetic than partisan, more spiritual than ideological. It is indeed time to call for a cease-fire in the culture wars—for the sake of our children.

Who speaks for God? God speaks for God. And it is the voiceless and powerless for whom the voice of God has always been authentically raised. It is up to us to make sure that our political vision bears some resemblance to the vision the prophets of God proclaim throughout the Scriptures. Then the people on the street corners will have a better idea of who the children of God really are.

Biblical religion could indeed help to morally reinvigorate politics, but not in the way the Religious Right suggests. As we have seen, religion has fostered moral political forces that helped to overcome slavery, secure civil rights, extend suffrage, defend workers, protect children, release prisoners, and gain freedom.

Today, we must stand ready, like the prophet Nehemiah, to "rebuild the wall" that has so badly crumbled in so many of our communities. But for that to work the political will, moral resolve, and human and economic resources must be mobilized to get the job done. No one must be allowed to opt out, from either the private or public sector, and the religious community could help lead the way. In Washington, on a sunny spring day in May, we said, "Let the building begin!" Now, in every community in the country, we hope the builders will come forward. Because there is good work to be done.

TWO

Compassion: The First Test of Politics

"It really isn't compassionate to take somebody's money and give it to somebody else. That's not compassionate. . . . And I don't think there's anything in the Constitution that says the government owes anybody welfare or a job or anything. The government does not owe grants of money to any group in our society."

On why Head Start is unnecessary: "If you're smart, you'll catch up anyway."

On President Bush's health-care voucher proposal: "You are guaranteed the poor will be stealing from it like they do food stamps and everything else."

"These girls are not stupid. If you want to pay them five hundred, six hundred, seven hundred, eight hundred dollars a month, or whatever it is, to have a baby, they'll have babies. And if they'll stop paying them, they'll stop having babies. It's that simple."

—Pat Robertson, *The 700 Club*

Compassion has less to do with "doing charity" than "making connections." The word *compassion* means lit-

erally "to suffer with." It means to put yourself in somebody else's shoes, try to understand their experience, or
see the world through their eyes. That always changes
our perspective. True compassion has less to do with
sympathy than it does with *empathy*.

The call to compassion is not about somebody "doing for" somebody else. Rather, its value is in the connection, the relationship, and the transaction in which
everyone is changed. The Hebrew prophets say that we
find our own good in seeking the common good. The
prophet Isaiah says that when we feed the hungry, take
in the homeless, and "break the yoke" of oppression,
then we will find *our own healing*. He also says the act
of compassion requires that you "not hide yourself from
your own flesh." In other words, *compassion* means to
recognize the kindred spirit we all share together. *And
the Bible insists that the best test of a nation's righteousness is how it treats the poorest and most vulnerable in
its midst.*

Isaiah in the Rotunda

Surrounded by the statues of Washington, Jefferson, and
King, fifty-five inner-city pastors intoned the words of
Isaiah,

"Woe to the legislators of infamous laws,
to those who issue tyrannical decrees,

who refuse justice to the unfortunate
who cheat the poor among my people of their
  rights,
who make widows their prey
and rob the orphan."

A group of schoolchildren were in the Rotunda of the U.S. Capitol taking a tour when the disruption occurred. The eighth-graders from Virginia stood transfixed and quickly moved as close as they could to our circle of ministers that had formed in the center of the historic Capitol dome. Capitol police also rushed over to loudly inform us through their bullhorns that no singing, praying, Scripture reading, or anything of the sort would be tolerated in this place.

Undeterred, the pastors continued. "God hears the cry of the poor!" was boldly proclaimed. The acoustics in the Capitol Rotunda are quite good and the religious message carried through the corridors to within earshot of the members of Congress who were at that very moment debating what to do about the poor. It was later revealed that Ralph Reed, executive director of the Christian Coalition, was just down the hall in a closed-door meeting with Newt Gingrich, the Republican speaker of the House.

Most of the urban church leaders had come from around the country, where each one works every day in ministries of compassion—with at-risk kids on the street, single mothers, men and women laid off their jobs, homeless people, families without health care, those struggling to overcome addictions, people dying from AIDS, senior citizens, refugees with nowhere to go, and children with all kinds of problems. They had interrupted their important daily work to come to Washington because of what was about to happen to the people they care about. With the schoolchildren, tourists, police, and reporters looking on, the men and women in clerical garb turned to Isaiah again:

"The Lord enters into judgment
with the elders and princes of his people;
It is you who have devoured the vineyard;
the spoil of the poor is in your houses.
What do you mean by crushing my people,
by grinding the face of the poor?
Says the Lord God of Hosts."

If we have been fiscally irresponsible as a nation, why are we blaming the poor? If we have spent too much money on weapons and war, why are we blaming those who need the most protection? If we have been too generous with large public subsidies to big corporations, why are we blaming the people at the bottom? And if the welfare systems we have set up are not working very well, why are we blaming the recipients? Why is it that the poor, and especially poor women and children, will bear the biggest brunt of budget balancing and deficit reduction, instead of the Pentagon, the *Fortune* 500, and the middle class? Does this seem fair to anyone? Would this seem fair to God?

To make things worse, it was the season of Advent, just a few weeks before Christmas 1995. The season of "peace and goodwill on earth" is usually a time that calls all of us to greater compassion for the poor and downtrodden. Yet the Congress had picked this holy season to especially focus on cutting the public resources that go to the weakest, poorest, and most vulnerable citizens in the land. The politicians had reversed the intent of the old slogan in their deficit cutting; when they got out their budget cutters, it was "women and children first."

As evangelical, Catholic, black, and Latino pastors, we went to the Capitol because the poor had no voice or clout there, no high-paid lobbyists to make sure that they escape the ax of budget cutting that more powerful interests have successfully avoided. Neither side in the Congressional debate got off easily from the urban pastors who came to Washington. *The New York Times* reported that the ministers, in prophetic style, "lambasted Republicans and Democrats alike for variously demonizing and bureaucratizing the poor."

One by one we were handcuffed and led away to jail. The singing, praying, and Scripture reading continued until the last pastor and church worker was taken out of the Rotunda. At that moment the schoolchildren and tourists burst into applause in support of the demonstrators. Afterward, National Public Radio interviewed the kids, who said they had learned something that day about "unity," about "standing up for what you believe," and about "courage." The children said they thought it was good to speak up for people in need and that the pastors had gotten their point across.

In the midst of the debate gripping the nation's Capitol, a voice of prophetic outrage must be lifted up, along with a clear moral vision of new possibilities. That prophetic voice must not simply defend old systems and approaches that have failed to transform poverty and sometimes have further entrenched it. But it must clearly say that the poor, and especially our children, must not be punished for the welfare system's failures. We must find another way, and bring a new moral dimension to the public debate at both the national level and in every local community.

The preachers proclaimed a prophetic biblical word and prayed for the poor in the face of their assailants. But offering more than a protest, they also gave an invitation. All of them are deeply involved in their own local communities to create the new approaches the nation sorely needs. They not only raised up an alternative vision, but actually represented it. The religious leaders called the nation's political leaders to repentance—to seek new solutions together, to find common ground, and to protect the poor.

A new approach to the alleviation of poverty in America is critically needed. But *it is absolutely immoral to slash and burn old systems and safety nets with nothing new to replace them.* The children's schoolteacher in the Rotunda told *The New York Times* she was "ashamed" of her government for withdrawing support of the basic human needs of its people.

A Budget Is a Moral Document

Many Americans agree with that eighth-grade teacher. A budget is also a moral document, and the morality of further benefiting the rich while balancing the budget on the backs of the poor, the young, and the old is simply unacceptable.

The biblical text from the Gospel of Matthew that Congressman Poshard quoted in his House speech on welfare policy was indeed relevant. This Scripture is often used as a religious test of those who claim to be followers of Jesus—"As you have done to the least of these, you have done to me." But it also serves as a good test of politics from a religious perspective.

In the passage, Jesus names the categories of persons most easily forgotten or stigmatized, then dramatically identifies himself with their plight. He speaks of the hungry and thirsty—those masses of people, especially children, who inhabit the refugee camps, squatter communities, and urban ghettos where life is an everyday struggle for survival. He speaks of the stranger—the alien, immigrant, the outsider who is always feared or blamed. He speaks of the naked—the vulnerable who are without the protection of clothing, shelter, or social systems. He speaks of the sick—those whose ill health makes every aspect of life more painful, difficult, and fearful. He speaks of the imprisoned—those who have broken society's laws and are in danger of being forever written off. All these are in jeopardy in any society, and Jesus insists that they not be abandoned. He insists that we make connection to them.

Imagine if Jesus were to just show up at one of those budget-cutting sessions in the U.S. Congress. The legislators might be quite surprised as they looked up from their busy work to see a poorly dressed character in the doorway of their committee room.

"I was hungry. . . ." he says. "Well, we had to balance the budget," they reply.

"I was thirsty. . . ." Earnestly they explain, "We had to cut somebody's programs to reduce the deficit."

He quietly continues, "I was naked. . . ." Shifting uneasily in the chairs now, the politicians answer, "Maybe fending for themselves will help the poor to build character."

He goes on, "I was a stranger. . . ." They retort,

"Well, from now on only U.S. citizens will be entitled to any social benefits."

Looking them straight in the eyes he tells them, "I was sick. . . ." On the defensive now, they respond, "If you do get sick, you're just going to have to pay more to get well."

Finally, he says to the politicians, "I was in prison. . . ." Brightening up, they answer, "Well, you're in luck there because we are going to build a lot more prisons."

The homeless-looking figure sadly turns and departs, concluding as he leaves, "As you have done to the least of these, you have done to me."

We tend to demonize the poor, the outsider, the marginal, the homeless, the unemployed, the pregnant teenager, the illegal immigrant, the addicted, the one caught up in unfortunate circumstances—especially if their behavior becomes the least bit antisocial or disruptive. What has happened to them must be mostly their fault, we defensively conclude. That helps us feel less responsible for their plight. Compassion does not seem to come very easily to us as human beings. The old expression *There but for the grace of God go I*, is one that we quite quickly forget.

Compassion is a requirement of good religion, and it is also a good test of politics. Why? Because it is the potentially marginalized who are the best test of any society's understanding of community. If those on the edges can be banished from our boundaries of concern, then we are all potentially in danger. But if even the weakest and most vulnerable have a place within the political ways we define community, then we will all be assured of having our own place. Compassion creates a safe place for us all.

When Pope John Paul II visited America, in the midst of the 1995 budget debates, he focused on compassion and the American spirit. "The same spirit of generosity will help you to meet the needs of your own poor and disadvantaged. They, too, have a role to play in building a society truly worthy of the human person—a society in which none are so poor that they have nothing to give and none are so rich that they have nothing to receive."

Compassion is about "making connections" with each other, especially across the deep social chasms that separate us. It is how we make those connections with one another that this society so desperately needs to learn.

The War of the Elites

Recently, a delegation of congresspeople visited a little church not far from where I live in Washington, D.C. Most admitted they had never spoken to a homeless person before or even had a serious discussion with a black American (these congresspeople were all white). The pastor gave them an afternoon's tour of the church's ministries and of other church-based projects in our area.

The members of Congress were all very impressed, especially with the after-school programs for children, the housing construction for low-income home buyers, and an array of new community-based economic-development initiatives in our section of the city.

"We are really supportive of all these wonderful efforts," one of them exclaimed after the tour was finished.

"No, I don't think you are," answered the pastor politely.

More than a little startled, the politicians asked him what he meant. The inner-city minister told them they had voted against the very tax credits and other funding that helped make these hopeful community gains possible.

"What we opposed goes to support all this?" they asked incredulously.

"Absolutely," replied the pastor.

"Well . . . I guess we had better reexamine our policies, then," said one of the congressmen.

"Absolutely," said the preacher.

A policy war between political elites is occurring at the top levels of power in Washington, D.C., and the primary casualties will be poor children who live at the bottom of this society. Republicans and Democrats are locked in a bitter political confrontation, from which few are really looking for a way out.

The current welfare debate offers a false choice between unsatisfactory alternatives. In order to meet their goals of spending and tax cuts, conservative Republicans have ended up targeting our poorest and most vulnerable citizens to bear the brunt of deficit reduction. At the same time, the Republican Congress proposes to give more money to the Pentagon than it has even asked for, despite the major role military spending played, during the 1980s, in creating the huge budget deficit we now have. A few Republican deficit hawks, even Budget Committee chairman John Kasich, have urged the cutting of expensive weapons systems like the B-2 bomber and the Seawolf submarine, but their pleas have fallen on deaf ears.

The Republicans have also loyally preserved "corporate welfare" (all of the many government subsidies and tax breaks that go to big business) while determinedly cutting resources that go to poor women and children. The corporate lobbyists whom Colin Powell has dubbed as the "welfare kings on K Street" have all blessed the current budget proposals, which cut and cap everything except their own benefits and entitlements.

While McDonald's will get more tax dollars to subsidize their advertising of Chicken McNuggets in Europe, single mothers with kids will somehow have to get by with less, and senior citizens on tight fixed incomes will have to pay more for their medical care. The wealthiest Americans will be getting by with more, as they will be the biggest beneficiaries of the tax breaks being proposed by the Republicans along with their budget cuts. Most Americans know that the nation's welfare system needs some very basic changing, but they're uncomfortable with leaving the poor just to fend for themselves.

For their part, however, the Democrats have failed to offer any real alternative vision to current welfare policies. Time and time again they have failed to reform the system when they had a chance to do so, most recently in President Clinton's first term. It is now undeniably and painfully true that, despite their intentions, large and distant bureaucracies have too often created more dependency than opportunity, more control than caring, and more stories of wasteful inefficiency than personal and family success. The moribund welfare system has long cried out for transformation and a completely new approach.

But the Democrats have mostly defended old institutions that, while not winning the war on poverty, still provided a political base for themselves. Wedded to old approaches and vested constituencies, the Democrats have long been mere defenders of the status quo. And they, too, have not been very willing to take on the powerful interests behind military expenditures and corporate welfare.

That failure at reform is resulting in disaster as the

Republicans now seek to simply dismantle the old with nothing new to take its place. Change—and fundamental change—is desperately needed in the way that we approach the whole complex of issues around poverty, including: the failures of the welfare system itself; the social disintegration of family and community; the corporate downsizing, loss of jobs, and decline in real wages throughout a changing global economy; continued racism and the assaults upon positive personal and social values from the media and the popular culture. All these factors combine in ways that particularly devastate the lives of poor people, and especially children.

New approaches and strategies are urgently needed. To be effective they must be based in local communities, be focused on the need for better values, take family building as seriously as community organizing, create jobs as well as self-esteem, and, above all, they must favor solutions over slogans. Neither party seems to have any real vision for that.

The new local strategies we need cannot depend only upon government programs, which the Democrats have preferred, nor can they simply "dump" the problem onto churches and charities as Republican leaders have suggested. *The New York Times* recently estimated that for churches to take up the slack of cut government aid to the poor, each church in America would have to increase its budget by $250,000 per year. That's more than the whole budget of many churches and would add an enormous amount to the burden of most others.

A Religious Witness

The witness in the Rotunda was not a partisan statement, but a religious one, with a voice dramatically different from that of the Religious Right. The Christian Coalition has been among the loudest voices *in favor* of cutting funds for poor women and children and, in fact, for the elimination of all public support for those in need. Welfare mothers were actually vilified at the Coalition's 1995 "Road to Victory" Conference as irresponsible people who live in nice apartments, sit in Jacuzzis, sell food stamps for money to buy drugs, dump their kids in government-run day care centers, and then spend the day at the beach. It is amazing how the leaders of the Religious Right, who generally live far away from the poor, are such experts on their behavior.

At the Christian Coalition's national gathering, the worse the caricatures of the poor became, the louder was the applause from the virtually all-white middle-class audience of fundamentalist Christians. After hearing the diatribes against the poor, these politicized Christians were off to lunch at lovely Washington restaurants around their hotel and, reportedly, completely ignoring scores of homeless people in the rush to get there—a sight that would no doubt have made Jesus proud of the ways His children were bringing "Christian values" back to America.

It is ironic, and indeed quite tragic, that the tremendous increase in the political power of Christians, through the organizing of the Religious Right, has not served to benefit the poor and oppressed, but instead has actually *hurt* them.

In La Mesa, California, a local Christian Coalition chapter opposed a program to feed schoolchildren, even though one quarter of the children were poor enough to qualify for the supplemental food. Christian Coalition member Donald J. Smith attacked the food program as "one more example of government interference in family life." The Religious Right leader proclaimed, "We shouldn't take away parental responsibility."

What does that mean to the parents of poor families desperately trying to feed their children? The radical-Right-dominated school board of Vista, California, actually turned down a $400,000 federal grant to provide social services in the district schools. Capturing local school boards is one of the primary strategies of the Christian Coalition and the Religious Right. And their agenda in local communities involves far more than fighting abortion. They intend to impose a radical right-wing agenda, which, among other things, will be very bad news to poor and marginalized people.

Fortunately, the Religious Right is not the only Christian voice on these matters. At the U.S. Catholic Bishops

Conference meeting in the fall of 1995, a very different note was sounded in the face of threatened Congressional budget cuts.

Roger Cardinal Mahony of Los Angeles called upon his fellow bishops to depart from their prearranged agenda, in light of the urgency of the situation, and to decry "the current unprecedented dismantling by Congress of essential health-care, educational, and social service programs." The cardinal called the Republican-driven changes "an extraordinary assault upon the poorest members of our society" and on "immigrant brothers and sisters, and various minority groups."

The next day the bishops issued a pastoral letter to every member of Congress asking them to "reject this fatally flawed legislation. . . . While the language is reform, the reality is cutting resources and shifting responsibilities." The cumulative effect of the changes being proposed "will be devastating to poor and working families," the bishops' letter said.

It wasn't long before the Christian Coalition announced that it was forming an auxiliary group called the "Catholic Alliance," clearly intended to counter the Catholic bishops on political matters. The Catholic Alliance is now labeling the Bishops Conference as pro-Democratic and pro-Clinton, despite the real differences the bishops have with a traditional liberal agenda. Their intent is less to change the content of the Catholic bishops' teaching on social matters, than it is to intimidate and hopefully mute the bishops' voice in the political debate.

Time for a Fresh Conversation

It is time for a fresh conversation about what to do about the poor. We need a new debate on welfare, in the Congress and in local communities around the country, to really open up the discussion. For too long liberals and conservatives have been simply blaming the other side for the poverty and violence that have grown out of control.

As I write, a fourteen-year-old has just shot another teenager in the lobby of Cardozo High School, two blocks from where I live. And there are stories like that virtually every week. Several months ago, I came home from a meeting at the White House about urban violence only to find that, *while we were meeting,* another young man had been killed across the street from my house. The now infamous and painfully familiar yellow tape the police put on the concrete around the place the dead body has fallen was there to greet me upon my return. (I've often wondered, if more people in those kinds of meetings came home to yellow tape in the streets where their own children play, whether something might finally be done.)

What can we now agree on, and where do the real issues lie? Government has indeed grown too big and bureaucratic—too removed from ordinary citizens, including the poor. The impulse for compassion has sometimes paradoxically given rise to government programs that have a more harsh than human face. And we must conclude sadly that, for too many, welfare has become a way of life that results in dependency and despair, rather than another chance up and out of a life cycle of poverty.

In regard to welfare reform, many Americans are unhappy with long lines of people waiting for a social worker, but are also uncomfortable with the social Darwinism of the new Republican Congress. New solutions, preferably at the local level and which involve public/private alliances to solve a range of problems—from poverty, youth violence, and drug addiction to unemployment, housing, and education—are not only possible, but are being seriously experimented with around the nation.

Compassion is not a soft and sloppy concept that replaces the need for individual responsibility. Nor should compassion be the excuse for endlessly justifying social systems that are not working. It would indeed be prudent to require more personal responsibility from those on welfare. It clearly should not encourage permanent dependency, but rather offer help in the transition toward work and stability in a time of trouble. The incentives against work and the rules that tend to break up two-parent families in the present welfare system have been a disaster and should be eliminated.

Encouraging welfare mothers, especially teenage ones, to take better care of their children and themselves (through requiring school attendance, medical care, job training, and so on) is also a reasonable step. So is discouraging further out-of-wedlock births, as long as it doesn't punish the children, who have nothing to do with their parents' behavior. Forcing deadbeat dads to assume financial responsibility for their children is a critical measure as well. But positive change will not happen if we are oblivious of shrinking opportunities for low-skilled employment and continue to scale back child care, job training, and medical coverage.

The primary purpose of welfare reform must be to move people from welfare to work, not to save money in the short term. That's because the support services needed to effect successful welfare-to-work transitions may, in the experience of several states, cost more, in the short run, than current welfare expenditures. Long term, such policies are a very good social investment, but they cannot be relied upon for immediate deficit reduction or budget relief.

Budget balancing must come from other places, but isn't that as it should be? Why should the poor be the ones to bail us out of our fiscal problems? Cuts can be found in military spending, "corporate welfare," and from "means testing" the affluence of those who receive more middle- and upper-middle-class entitlements (like Social Security, which is now "off the table" for both political parties). These kinds of budget cuts would be more effective and fair in reducing the deficit. But here both compassion and sound public policy fly in the face of the political realities of various constituencies' political clout. And since the poor have no clout, they are the most vulnerable constituency.

But even if the taxing and spending policies of Washington were just and equitable, they would not be enough to provide our society with the solutions we now need in response to our proliferating social crisis. Indeed, what we require is a new spirit of compassion, mobilized on the community level.

A "Gang Summit"

I often begin discussions on compassion by talking about the young gang members in the streets, because that's who America is most afraid of. We don't feel toward them as we do toward Jean Valjean in *Les Misérables,* who stole a loaf of bread to feed his sister's children and got nineteen years in prison for it. We don't have the same sympathy for them that we do for a young Jewish girl on a donkey who had to deliver her first child in an animal stall because there was no room for them in the inn. But there *wasn't* room for them in the inn, and Valjean's criminal stigma followed him around for the rest of his life.

Working with these young people over the last several

years has been very instructive to me. Often when I'm just sitting around with these street kids, I'm struck by two things at the same time: These are the people America is most frightened of *and* they seem so very vulnerable and afraid.

Oh, they're tough, and many of them are capable of horrendous violence. But underneath the tough exterior are young people who have been abandoned and deeply hurt by a lack of love and connection. Indeed, that is what drew many of them to the gangs in the first place, along with their need for an economic livelihood. The lack of love and family is what they talk about themselves when they are in an environment in which they're comfortable enough to speak honestly.

Recently, I was in Washington State, for a "gang summit" in Spokane. This sleepy, middle-size town of 300,000 people had become the scene of fierce gang warfare, drive-by shootings, and growing public fear. A gang peace summit is an occasion to bring everybody together. Often convened by the religious community, as this one was, the summits gather together city officials, pastors, parents, neighborhood organizations, media, the police, and, most critically, the young gang members themselves. It is a time to *listen* to one another's stories, and try to reach some better understanding of each other and of what is happening in the community.

Always the most moving time is when the young people tell their own stories to the rest of the community. In Spokane young boys and girls with their baseball caps on backward, wearing bandannas, earrings, and baggy pants, each told how they had gotten lost in the midst of social and cultural breakdown.

Of course, they didn't use those words. Instead they spoke of how their family had broken up, or how their only parent was an alcoholic or drug addict, or how the streets became their home and the gang their surrogate family, or how they could never get an education or find a good job, or how they, as the song goes, had been "looking for love in all the wrong places."

These "testimonies" are, of course, always wrenching and deeply moving. And I'm always amazed when the fears of a community turn into communal tears as citizens hear the stories of the young people in their town who have just gotten lost in the cracks. As our cracks have become gaping social chasms, more and more of our young people are getting lost. Los Angeles, where the modern gang movement began, now reports 110,000 young people in gangs.

Sitting there before us in Spokane were red, black, brown, and white young people showing the rainbow of our problems and our possibilities. When asked by adults in the room what their hopes and dreams were, Shawn said he wanted to go to college and study "youth ministry." Sonny, a Native American and natural leader, wanted to keep writing poetry and to study music so he could follow his first love of songwriting. A young woman who had survived both abuse at home and rape on the streets said she wanted to raise a family with the love she'd never had. Lee said he had already started that kind of family, but needed a good job to support his new wife and child. Angie said she dreamed of being a teacher to instill the right values in young people, but didn't know how she would ever afford an education. And Dar said that the first thing many kids needed was just a safe place to come and get off the streets in the afternoons and evenings.

The response was almost immediate. A young pastor, who had just come to town, said he had inherited a big church facility with a gymnasium and kitchen but almost no people. From now on, the minister said, his church would be open every day after school, and he hoped these young people might even help him start a new congregation. An amazing couple who had been taking in young gangsters off the street for several years were literally surrounded with support and questions about how other families could open up their homes too. The dean, chaplain, and several faculty members from the university where I had spoken the previous day showed up for the gang summit. They quickly arranged a tour of the campus for all of those young people really interested in pursuing an education, and privately assured me that scholarships would be made available for those ready to make a commitment.

Several veteran activists and businesspeople began discussing the possibilities of community-based economic development. A former police officer was very insightful about the kind of community support and accountability that cops need to play a more helpful role in the problems of youth violence. City and county commissioners who run addiction programs were swapping phone numbers with local pastors and some of the young people in the hope of becoming more effectively involved in the community. The three television stations and local newspaper who covered the day's events were challenged to report honestly and constructively rather than sensationally about youth, gangs, and violence. And the citizens of Spokane were now ready to challenge their city, state, and federal government to play a more positive leadership role in solving the problems we had discussed, and to do their part, along with others, in finding the necessary resources for the job.

Compassion grew into strategy that day in Spokane, and the next meetings were eagerly planned. In the words of Isaiah, those gathered hoped to be "repairers of the breach" and "restorers of streets to dwell in." Everybody was at the table, which will make the strategies far more effective. The whole community was involved in the listening and the talking, and is now much more likely to be engaged in the solutions.

It is certain that what is needed in our ravaged inner cities and impoverished rural areas today is beyond just

what the government can do. This will take all of us—
our families, churches, and communities. It will test our
moral resolve and political will, and require both the
private and public sector to become involved in new and
creative ways. No one gets to opt out.

The young people in Spokane were included that day
of the gang summit. And from the many hopeful comments made by so many members of the Spokane community, I believe anyone who was there on that momen-
tous November Saturday with these young people
would now feel safe with them.

Getting Mugged

Some political commentators like to say that "a conservative is a liberal who has been mugged." Well, I got
mugged last year, and it just showed me again how
much our social crisis has been the result of a failure of
compassion.

It finally happened. After more than two decades of
living and working in many of America's meanest
streets, I was mugged. As a veteran urban pastor, orga-
nizer, and even a gang truce adviser, I'm embarrassed to
say that they took me by surprise. It was only six
o'clock in the evening—during rush hour. I suppose I
watch my back better after midnight. But these guys
were so fast and bold, I'm not sure it would have made
any difference.

Needing a few things at the store before an early-morning flight, I headed out to my pickup truck parked right around the corner from where I live in Washington, D.C.'s Fourteenth Street corridor. I wasn't paying much attention.

Ironically, I was about to travel to Seattle and speak to a retreat for the mayor and his cabinet and staff on "politics and values." The topic was on my mind when I heard running feet behind me.

Looking over my shoulder, I saw four young men bearing down on me. The first one hit my slightly turned head with something sharp enough to open a gash above my left eye. The force of the blow and a push from two others sent me to the pavement. One of them yelled, "Keep him down! Get his wallet!" It finally registered. These guys were trying to roll me over.

I popped up quickly, which seemed to surprise them. Seeing no weapons flashed, I squared to face my attackers. This was the first chance we had to really see each other face to face. I saw that my assailants were just children—three about fifteen, and one little one who couldn't have been more than thirteen. I didn't know them, never having seen them on the street before, and they didn't know who I was either.

The boys backed up a little when they saw I was bigger than they had expected. I'm a strong believer in nonviolence, but have learned that being a weightlifter often helps in these potential conflict situations! The one who had hit me moved into a boxing stance while the others circled. The little guy began attempting some ineffectual karate kicks, which I assumed he had seen on television.

I decided to confront them, not intending to hurt them, but only to fend them off. Instinctively I began to scold these lost young souls. I told them just to stop it, to stop terrorizing people, to stop such violent behavior in our neighborhood. Finally I shouted at them, "I'm a pastor!" And I told them if they wanted to try to beat up and rob a pastor, they should come ahead and take their best shot.

Maybe it was my desire to confront these kids with what they were doing and give a personal identity to their potential victim. I don't think the young stalkers who prowl our streets usually confront the reality of what they are doing or who they're doing it to. But I knew that invoking the authority of the church in the street is hardly a sure thing these days, when our churches often have such little involvement there.

Whatever it was that changed their minds, the youthful muggers turned and ran. "Get back here," I shouted after them—then instantly realized it probably wasn't a good thing to say at that moment. But then something unusual happened.

The littlest kid, who couldn't have been more than four and a half feet tall, turned back and looked at me as he ran away. With a sad face and voice the young karate kicker said, "Pastor, ask God for a blessing for me."

He and his friends had just assaulted me. The little one had tried so hard to be one of the big tough guys. Yet he knew he needed a blessing. The young boy knew he was in trouble. I think they all did.

Compassion for Whom?

Let's be clear about some things here. These kids were dangerous. The social pathologies they demonstrate *are* a threat to the society. You're not likely to underestimate their danger or romanticize the poverty of young perpetrators when they have just hit you over the head, as some socially concerned liberals who live at a safe distance from them sometimes do. These kids intended to rob me and were willing to hurt me, or worse, to do so.

Let's take it a step further. Perhaps these kids come from single-parent families on welfare. I don't know that for a fact, but since it is true of *most* families in my neighborhood and even more true of the backgrounds of kids who get into gangs and street crime, it's a pretty safe bet. If it's true, the bloody wound on my head was another indication that the welfare state isn't working very well.

Driving to the doctor to get stitched up, I was especially conscious of other people out walking, many just coming home from work, and most more vulnerable than I am on the street. So many potential victims of my gang of four. All these people deserve to be safe on the streets of their own neighborhoods and city. *That* must be a bottom line to which we commit ourselves. Freedom from fear on the streets where we live is a very important element to the quality of life in a democracy.

But what about those kids? Are they just perpetrators and little social pathologies whom we should give up on, cut off, and lock away? That's what the current political rulers in Washington seem to think, as do their religious chaplains in the Christian Coalition. Or are they our children too—children who have lost their way? Who will show compassion for them?

Does their dysfunctional and violent behavior reveal only their crisis, or does it expose ours as well? Do we really have a "youth crisis," or is it a societal crisis of which young people bear the brunt? Indeed, our young people are often the scapegoats of our social crisis. Is their problem that they haven't gotten the values of the larger society, or is the problem that they have?

When will we commit ourselves to those kids? When will they also become our bottom line? What those young people need most is nurture, discipline, and a real opportunity. Most of them have had none of those. And as long as they don't, our streets will continue to grow more dangerous.

Compassion for victims of street crime has become a

bigger and bigger issue for me as so many members of my church community have been assaulted and robbed in the neighborhood. Several months after I was attacked, one of our young intern volunteers had a similar experience. Since arriving to work in the neighborhood, she had already been mugged twice. On this occasion she was carrying her laundry down the street when three kids no more than ten or eleven rushed into her, demanded her money, and began to go through her backpack.

By this time she was tired of all this and told them exactly what she thought. She angrily said she had been mugged before and now didn't carry any money. She told them that she had come to live and volunteer in this neighborhood, to get along with people, and help make it a better place. And she scolded her rude young assailants for treating people this way. "If you need something, ask for it," she reprimanded them, "but don't just take things from other people."

Having gotten only a pack of cigarettes, the kids fled. But then one came back, put his arms around her, and just hugged her for the longest time. He kept saying he was sorry and she could hardly peel him off her. Then the other two returned, held out her cigarettes, and asked her if they could have one. "I normally wouldn't give a cigarette to a kid," she told me, "but in this case I thought I should—they were learning to ask." Standing there on the street, the four of them had a very good talk together.

Every night in my neighborhood young people demonstrate the social pathologies that make them a very real threat. Yet they themselves are also vulnerable and alone, as these two encounters showed. How do we rebuild the relationships, the structures, and the environments that provide the essentials of life for our young people?

The current Washington rhetoric of "three strikes and you're out" won't do it. And neither will that ugly phrase failed Republican presidential candidate Phil Gramm repeated ad nauseam: "It's time for those people who have been riding in the wagon to get out and help the rest of us pull it!" That may be as clear a statement as we have on the public record which directly rails against compassion. (Of course, we all know Senator Gramm means poor people on welfare, and not the Texas fat cats he so ably represents, who, with the help of politician friends like him, have been feeding at the government trough for years.)

Senator Sam Nunn of Georgia spoke directly to the question of compassion as he addressed the 1996 National Prayer Breakfast in Washington, D.C., with a moving story.

"I recently heard a story on the radio. A reporter was covering that tragic conflict in the middle of Sarajevo, and he saw a little girl shot by a sniper. The reporter threw down his pad and pencil, and stopped being a reporter for a few minutes. He rushed to the man who was holding the child, and helped them both into his car.

"As the reporter stepped on the accelerator, racing to the hospital, the man holding the bleeding child said, 'Hurry, my friend, my child is still alive.'

"A moment or two later, 'Hurry, my friend, my child is still breathing.'

"A moment later, 'Hurry, my friend, my child is still warm.'

"Finally, 'Hurry. Oh, my God, my child is getting cold.'

"When they got to the hospital, the little girl had died. As the two men were in the lavatory, washing the blood off their hands and their clothes, the man turned to the reporter and said, 'This is a terrible task for me. I must go tell her father that his child is dead. He will be heartbroken.'

"The reporter was amazed. He looked at the grieving man and said, 'I thought she was your child.'

"The man looked back and said, 'No, but aren't they all our children?' "

"Yes, they are all our children. They are also God's children as well, and he has entrusted us with their care in Sarajevo, in Somalia, in New York City, in Los Angeles, in my hometown of Perry, Georgia, and here in Washington, D.C."

Perhaps the only thing more tragic than a child getting killed in a crossfire in a war in Sarajevo, is a child shot to death in a crossfire between two other armed children on the streets of an American city.

The violence must be stopped. The violent behavior of street criminals must be stopped. But the four young men who attacked me are more than just criminals. They are also children who belong to all of us, and they are in a great deal of trouble. The violence will only be turned around when the young people who now roam wild are included in our future. Young people who feel like they are part of a society's future will not be attacking the rest of us on the streets. If we can find the ways to include them, we will all receive a blessing.

A Civil Society

While community-based approaches like those being tried in Spokane are working around the country, the battle between old ideological approaches still rules in Washington, D.C. But even some in Washington are beginning to realize that the area in which new answers will emerge is what many are now calling "the civil society." Others call it the nonprofit sector, and it includes the full range of community, family, educational, religious, and civic organizations. Its energy is voluntary and, at its best, very creative.

In contrast to both liberal and conservative approaches, fresh solutions will almost certainly require new *partnerships* between nonprofit community organizations (both religious and nonreligious), the business sector, private foundations, *and* government on all levels. New configurations of people and groups must create new strategies and mobilize the resources (both public and private) to make them work. In many communities around the country new projects and partnerships with such vision are already under way.

New social visions must grow out of local communities joined in partnerships formed from all sectors of the society. While liberals have overrelied on the state for solutions to social problems, conservatives have relied too much on the market. Neither the state nor the market will, of themselves, produce the strategies and resources we now need. The new locally based strategies must involve everyone, because in that very involvement we might re-create the sense of community that we seem to have lost.

But for real solutions to emerge from the civil society, two things are necessary: First, there must be new and common strategies developed in every community to invite diverse people to work together. Second, the necessary resources must be found to do the job. Otherwise, the political talk of "privatizing" and bringing solutions back to local communities will ultimately just be a cover for abandoning the poorest in our midst and balancing the federal budget on the backs of inner-city children.

It is undeniably true that government alone cannot do what must be done. Many of the problems caused by a breakdown of family, community, and values cannot be solved only or even best by government action. But it is also true that "churches and charities" alone cannot possibly solve the enormous social problems we now confront.

Privatizing and localizing the response to poverty sounds like a good idea to many, but it is already-overstretched churches and community groups that will most feel the burden, and they cannot possibly carry it alone. All across the country creative and energetic groups and programs are demonstrating real solutions to our seemingly intractable problems. Specific examples will be cited later, but a close look at your own community will likely reveal programs along these lines. Many are church related and most of the successful ones combine an approach that is both value centered and community based, while committed to a spiritual vision of racial and economic justice. Most all of them are more personal, compassionate, effective—and far less costly—than comparable government programs. But almost all of these efforts are desperately struggling for their financial survival.

That is the *disconnect* in the new Washington rhetoric. The very people and groups who are doing what the conservative Republicans say ought to be done are fighting to find the resources to continue their work. The local, state, and federal governments must play a critical role both in helping to convene new partnerships and in mobilizing resources. The business community must also be called upon to play a much larger role in making critical resources and skills available for social change. If the rhetoric of moving the war on poverty to local religious and nonprofit organizations is put forward without the resources that are necessary, the conservative talk will be proven merely cynical and cruel—just another unfunded mandate. Is the populist Republican rhetoric real, or is it just code language for abandoning the poor? We shall see.

One powerful example of the approach we need is Christ House, a medical facility for the homeless poor in Washington, D.C., who are too sick to be on the street. A ministry of the Church of the Saviour, Christ House is personal, compassionate, transformational, and *cost effective*. It costs only $47 per day per person at Christ House, while the comparable services in the District of Columbia hospital system cost $700! Yet, when D.C. budget cutting began, it was the funds for Christ House (less than half of their budget) that were cut out. Now, that is just bad public policy. The Christ Houses and their counterparts who deal with a myriad of social problems in every neighborhood in this country should be multiplied across the land. And a funding partnership between government (local, state, and federal) and these nonprofit organizations—both religious and nonreligious—is the best way to solve many of our most pressing problems.

In our May 23, 1995, meeting with several religious leaders from the Call to Renewal, Newt Gingrich, the Republican speaker of the House, expressed the view that "the nonprofit sector must be revitalized, and its organizations become the instrumentalities of public policy." Later that same afternoon Democratic Senator Bill Bradley gave the same group an eloquent discourse that called for the "renewal of the civil society, whose institutions could become the delivery systems of government services." While the partisan polemics of Capitol Hill prevent a meeting of the minds between such politicians, the similarity in their expressed views points the way forward.

We must neither simply destroy welfare nor keep defending the welfare state. New community-based strategies that rely on the leadership of nonprofits in the civil society in partnership with both the public and business sectors could provide desperately needed alternatives. Instead of simply reacting to violence with more police, prisons, and capital punishment, we could commit ourselves to rebuilding the social and moral infrastructures that we know reduce crime, and to supporting the new ventures in criminal justice arrangements that have demonstrated their effectiveness in decreasing recidivism.

"We Got Some Ideas, Man!"

Barrios Unidos, based in northern California, is perhaps the most effective antiviolence organization working around the country in Latino barrios. Combining economic and spiritual development, the Barrios network now extends to more than twenty states. Homer Leíja, the twenty-one-year-old leader of Fresno's Barrios Unidos chapter, stayed in my house when he and other organizers were in town to support the development of a local Barrios chapter in Washington, D.C.

From midnight until three in the morning, Homer hosted his regular call-in radio show from my living room into poor barrios and prisons throughout northern California. His message was more than just ending violence, it was about young people turning their lives around and taking a leadership role in the transformation of their communities. "We've got some ideas, man," Homer told me. We need new ideas, and many of them are going to come from people like Homer. Are we ready to listen?

Joseph Marshall, Jr., a former high-school teacher who started the Omega Boys Club out of a schoolhouse basement—and whose *Street Soldiers* radio call-in program gives weekly advice and guidance to thousands of disenfranchised inner-city youth—has helped lead hundreds of young black men out of gang membership and drug dealing in the San Francisco Bay area, and helped put 120 of them through college. As he said to the Senate Subcommittee on Families, Drugs, and Alcoholism, "The success of the Omega Boys Club proves one thing loudly and clearly: Violence can be curbed, children's lives can be spared, and communities can be made safer, but only if—and this is a big if—only if we are willing to devote the time, the energy, and the personal and economic resources to making it happen. . . . It is not necessarily *they* who have given up on *us,* but *we* who have given up on *them.* The ball is in our court."

When the budget fight in Washington is finally over, the battle will shift to the states and to local communities. Official government reports show that the restructuring of the nation's welfare system could push over a million more children into poverty, depending upon which plans are ultimately followed. And the Children's Defense Fund estimates are even higher. Of particular danger is the possibility of a "race to the bottom" between states given "block grants" to replace federal welfare programs competing with each other for the lowest benefits to the poor, so as not to "attract them" and even to pressure them to go somewhere else.

If and when such changes occur, it will not be the time for churches and nonprofit organizations to hunker down for survival while we watch our communities sink further into poverty, despair, and violence. On the contrary it will be time for new leadership, especially from the religious community. It will be time to convene those new partnerships and configurations in every community around the country both to insist that the poor not be abandoned and to create a fresh approach. That new approach will depend on everyone's involvement.

It will call for a heightened level of volunteer activity from every sector of the society—both the energy of young people and the expertise of older generations. It will demand that businesses take much more responsibility for the communities in which they work and profit. It will need the strategic and collaborative investment of private foundations on national, regional, and local levels.

And it will require the active engagement of government—federal, state, and local—though perhaps in new ways. The nonprofit organizations, both religious and nonreligious, who have demonstrated they can get the job done need to be empowered and funded as public policy. Private-public partnerships must shape the strategies that will work for each community and then make sure that the resources are there to accomplish the necessary tasks. Republican and Democratic legislators must explore ways for government policy to do just that in supporting the nonprofit organizations whose leadership will be critical. Some are beginning to do so.

Because of their vocation to moral leadership and their universal presence throughout the country, churches and religious communities could play a catalytic role in developing such new partnerships and strategies. Indeed, they must. Not only would such involvement *not* violate the separation of church and state, it is vitally needed to infuse the social process with sorely lacking moral and spiritual values. In the areas of addictions and youth violence, for example, spiritually based approaches have proven far more effective than government programs by themselves.

Much is at stake, especially for those who are already most vulnerable. If the old paradigms and programs simply are destroyed, the chaos that would likely result would create even more suffering for those who already know the pain of being left behind.

One way or another the old welfare state is about to change. In too many instances the weeds of the welfare system have, over the years, grown to choke out healthy growth toward work, family, and stability. Senator Moynihan and a few other political leaders have repeatedly called for needed changes, but to no avail. The threat now is that the changes will be accomplished by bulldozer operators instead of gardeners.

If another vision and paradigm can now emerge in the ruins of the old structures, a whole new set of opportunities could result. The time has come to offer a new voice and a vision to construct new networks and models of community responsibility. And that responsibility belongs to all of us. It's a matter of compassion. And it's a test of who speaks for God.

THREE

Community: The Second Test of Politics

"The term black *really carries with it a militancy, doesn't it? There is something about it that is hard, that says, 'Man, we're going to get you.' "*
—Pat Robertson, *The 700 Club*

Community could become the touchstone for a new American politics. Because the longing for a deeper sense of community can be found among liberals, moderates, and conservatives, a new "communitarian ethic" may be the political vision that could help bring us together.

Bound Together

The moral and political foundation for community is that, fundamentally, *we need each other*. All our religious traditions teach that. Just as the natural world is an interconnected web of life, so is the human family "bound together and finely woven," as songwriter Ken

Medema sings. We are indeed our brother's and sister's keeper, which, in turn, is the only way that we will be kept safe and secure ourselves.

Martin Luther King, Jr., applied that spiritual principle to politics when he said, "Injustice anywhere is a threat to justice everywhere." And it was Martin Niemöller, a pastor in the German "confessing church," who uttered the now famous warning about the dangers of ignoring our responsibility to one another:

"In Germany the Nazis came for the Communists,
and I didn't speak up because I was not a Communist,
Then they came for the Jews,
and I didn't speak up because I was not a Jew,
Then they came for the labor unionists,
and I didn't speak up because I was not a labor unionist.
Then they came for the Catholics,
and I was a Protestant so I didn't speak up.
Then they came for me . . .
by that time there was no one to speak up for anyone.

In Jesus' parable of the "Good Samaritan" He cites a priest and a Levite who passed by a man who had been beaten and robbed, then left by the side of the road for dead. Those who ignored his plight, and passed by on the other side, were important and busy political and religious leaders. They all saw him, perhaps even felt some sympathy, but wouldn't spend the time or energy to become involved in helping the one in trouble. Finally, it was the Samaritan, of a different ethnic group and culture from both the victim and those who had already decided to pass him by, who stopped and aided the wounded victim. He took responsibility, bound up the man's wounds, took him to an inn where he could heal, and even provided his own financial resources to care for the man's needs. It was a picture, not only of compassion, but also of community. Which one, Jesus asks, was the good neighbor? Which one acted to keep the bonds of community intact?

Like the spirit of compassion, those bonds of community nurture and protect us all. Community provides a sense of belonging that every human being needs. It supplies the emotional and physical support that is necessary to sustain life. Community also creates the context for our economic livelihood and stability, the environment in which we can provide for ourselves, our family, and our responsibility to others. When community breaks down, we are all in trouble. The consequences of community breakdown will inevitably manifest themselves in dangerous social pathologies, and ultimately in violence.

The title of Hillary Rodham Clinton's book *It Takes a Village* derives from the old African proverb: Only a village can raise a child. More and more we are learning how true that really is. But the opposite is also painfully true: it takes a village to destroy a child. Today our villages—our communities—are not very friendly to children, and we are reaping the harvest of our neglect. Too many of us have "passed by on the other side" as in the parable of the Good Samaritan.

Fordham University's Dr. Beatrice Bruteau asks the right question: "How big is your *we*?" Can we expand our vision of community beyond our own skin, family, race, tribe, culture, country, and species? Spiritual life is more than what we believe, it also includes how we relate. Who is included in the *we* and who is not? That is both a spiritual and a political question. How we answer it will likely determine our future.

The Common Good

The biblical prophet Jeremiah made it clear that we find our own good in the good of the whole community. He exhorts each of us to "seek the welfare of the city" in which we find ourselves. For many years Catholic social teaching has stressed the central idea of the "common good." It is the sum total of all the conditions of our social life—economic, cultural, spiritual, and political. Those conditions must make it possible for men, women, and children to be protected and fulfilled in their basic humanity. Human rights and the dignity of the person are critical in all religious teaching. We are each made in the image of God, which gives every individual a fundamental worth.

As we approach the next millennium, the threats to community are increasing. The walls and chasms between us seem to be growing every day, and perhaps the most frightening thing is the number of people who appear to have given up on ever healing the breaches—especially our political leaders. Today politicians are much more likely to exploit our divisions than seek to overcome them. A serious commitment to bring people together across the racial, cultural, and economic divides doesn't even seem to be on the political agenda, much less near the top of it.

The barriers to community are both spiritual and political. To remove them as obstacles will indeed require political action but, even more deeply, a national renewal of our sense of community. That will most likely occur in local communities first. It is here that our old ideological categories are the most useless, and a new political conversation is required. Every day there is a battle for that new sense of community going on in neighborhoods, towns, and cities across the nation.

Perhaps the divisions that most threaten the fabric of American society today are those having to do with our racial divisions, our cultural wars, and the growing economic gaps between our citizens. During the 1992 election campaign a famous sign hung on the wall at Clinton campaign headquarters that said, IT'S THE ECONOMY, STUPID! Let's start there.

Wall Street and Main Street

In the New Hampshire presidential primary of 1996 Pat Buchanan shocked the nation and his own Republican party. Putting together a winning coalition of religious conservatives and disaffected workers, the former television commentator won a narrow victory over all his Republican rivals, including front-runner Bob Dole. He did so by injecting into the campaign the economic fears and insecurities that increasingly define the lives of many American families—issues that were scrupulously avoided by both the other Republicans and the Democrats.

The indisputable and dramatic growth in the gap between the nation's wealthy elites and *both* America's middle class and poor is the most neglected political fact in the country today—even though it is one of the most important. The American middle class is losing ground and hope for its children's future, and the poor are fighting for their very survival, while a small professional and business class reaps a whirlwind of unprecedented financial gain.

While the Republicans have perfected the message of an angry political populism targeting "big government," they have loyally protected the interests of the *Fortune*

500 companies as the party of "big business." This is the party's potentially fatal inconsistency—its Achilles' heel. As more and more people become castoffs of the new economy, and fear and insecurity spread throughout the middle class, "anticorporate" sentiment will continue to rise, along with the popular "antigovernment" hostility. The February 26, 1996, *Newsweek* cover displayed mug shots of some of the nation's top CEOs who have cut the jobs of thousands of workers in order to raise their stock prices, with the caption, "CORPORATE KILLERS."

To most people it just doesn't seem fair that while both productivity and corporate profits are going up, employees' wages and job security are going down. From 1979 to 1993 the economy grew by 35 percent, but in 1993 median household income was less than it had been in 1979, adjusted for inflation. While corporate profits and stock markets were soaring during that period, real incomes of the bottom 80 percent of Americans—yes, 80 percent—continued to fall. Between 1983 and 1989 the top 1 percent captured 62 percent of newly created wealth.

A January 1996 article in *The Wall Street Journal* led with the line "We're in the money." Entitled "Big Bonuses Likely for CEOs on Wall Street," the piece reported that bonuses and end-of-the-year compensation for the country's richest corporate executives could be higher than ever. CEO salaries in the U.S. are now often a hundred times more than what the entry-level employ-ees in their companies receive, a gap several times greater than just twenty or thirty years ago.

And salaries aren't all the chief executives get. "A number of these people have received very large grants of stock over the years, and the bull market benefits them in two ways," said a source for the *Wall Street Journal* article. "It improves their cash compensation and the value of their stock." The story went on to ex-claim, "What a golden age this is for corporate manag-ers. International competition has helped to hold down compensation costs for many companies, thus pushing up profits." That same day the *International Herald Tribune* reported that AT&T's decision to eliminate forty thousand jobs drew applause from Wall Street in-vestors and prompted another rise in the company's stock value.

The rapidly growing economic gaps between us have been among the best kept secrets of American politics. Whether or not they are aware of the extent of the deep-ening class divisions in our country, most Americans feel it down deep in their souls and in their pocket-books. Meantime, those who are the beneficiaries of the widening gulf are not anxious to have a public discus-sion about it.

There are some simple facts that no one really dis-putes, even though they are very rarely talked about. From about 1950 until about 1978 most all American families saw real growth in their income, with even the poorest families seeing growth. That long-term trend changed dramatically in the period from 1979 to the mid–nineteen nineties, when only the families in the top income brackets saw real growth. While deep income disparity is a historical fact of American life (income distribution had remained relatively unchanged since 1910), those gaps are now widening. The richest 5 percent of American households have seen their share of national income grow by about one quarter over the past two decades, but average workers feel the pinch in paychecks that are growing much more slowly, or not at all.

Republican leaders and their religious advisors suggest that those who talk this way are fomenting "class warfare" and proclaim that the "free market" will solve all problems. The complaint might come from one of the GOP incoming freshman class of the House and Senate, one quarter of whom are worth over $1 million, or maybe from one of the television preachers of the Religious Right, like Pat Robertson, whose immense personal fortunes are seldom discussed on their TV shows. Makes you wonder why Jesus talked more about money than any other issue, and why the rich of his day thought his ideas about sharing and community to be dangerously close to class warfare as well.

Into the political silence from Republican and Democratic party elites about the economic direction of the country, Buchanan threw a bomb when he attacked the "big boys" who are doing in the "little guys." Others like Jesse Jackson, Ralph Nader, Ross Perot, and Bill Bradley have also invoked the populist theme. But Buchanan's rhetoric is belligerent and inflammatory, and he often adds racial and ethnic communities to his blame list.

Commentator Kevin Phillips is very sympathetic to the populist critique but adds that "the promotion of man-in-the-street economics all too often results in the inflaming of man-in-the-street prejudices." But Phillips also points out the possibilities of a new populism beyond the present "duocracy" of the Republican and Democratic parties.

"Be Like Mike"

I recently encountered an extraordinary piece of information that sent me reeling, a statistic that became a startling metaphor for what is happening to us.

Michael Jordan has been paid more money in one year by Nike than all the workers in all the factories who make Nike shoes in Indonesia—all of them combined. It seems that Nike moved its factories out of South Korea when wages there began to rise. Indonesia's government has a history of using its armed forces to harshly suppress union organizers, which tends to keep wages low. So the mostly women and children who actually make Nike's shoes, *all together*, make less than Michael does for making his Nike commercials.

Is any one person worth that much more than so many others? There is a purely economic answer to the question that Nike has already decided. But there is a theological and spiritual question here too. What does it mean when we say that all the world's children are made in the image of God? Does that have any practical meaning for economics? There is a political question here as well. What does it do to political society when some people are valued so much more highly than others? Or when a very few have so much more influence and access to power than everybody else? Putting the question another way, what are the economic requirements for political community?

The growing polarization we find in America today is occurring all over the world. The Nike sweatshops and places like them are now rampant throughout the Third World as multinational corporations pick up their factories and relocate them in places with cheap labor and few environmental or safety standards. The results strike home in two ways.

First, Americans lose their jobs after generations of worker loyalty to big companies. I grew up in Detroit, Michigan, and saw jobs all of a sudden disappear—jobs that had been passed down from father to son for as long as people could remember. It is painful to watch whole communities like Flint, Michigan, be destroyed when powerful corporations like General Motors decide they no longer have any use for a community or its families. Why isn't that raised as a "family values" issue by the Republicans and the Religious Right?

Second, a new class of exploited workers is created, and environmental degradation often follows when the multinationals relocate to benefit from lack of unions, safety standards, or environmental regulations. These low-wage workforces are often predominantly women and children, reflecting a global pattern of both gender and generational exploitation.

What Would Jeremiah or Amos Say?

Until the 1980s, economic growth benefited most American families, including the poorest. But in the last decade and a half the rich have gotten much richer, the middle class has lost ground, and the poor have suffered the most. The startling fact that more people are in poverty now than at any time in the last thirty years, and that about half of them are children, barely makes a blip in *USA Today*.

Wouldn't such a social catastrophe have awakened the passion of biblical prophets like Jeremiah or Amos? We can find some clues to the health of a community from, of all places, biblical archaeology! Those who dig down into the ancient layers of civilization in Israel have made an interesting discovery. There are periods of time where the remains of the houses suggest that they were all about the same size, and the instruments of life reveal a certain equality of lifestyle. That evidence corresponds to times in biblical history when the voice of the prophets was relatively quiet. On the other hand, during the times when archaeological evidence shows great disparity among the sizes of houses and the instruments of life, the Hebrew prophets thundered about the judgment and justice of God. The gaps between us undermine community, polarize society, and rend the social fabric. And they seem to be a great concern to God.

The gaps that awakened the prophetic anger of the biblical sages would pale in comparison to the huge divides that separate us today. Yet, most of the churches are sleeping through the crisis, while the Religious Right lauds the virtues of corporate business, preaches a "prosperity theology" to its wealthy donors, lectures the poor about their personal responsibilities, and fights to extend tax relief to America's wealthiest families. (The Christian Coalition fought to expand tax breaks to those families making up to $200,000 per year, instead of the $80,000 salary cap others were suggesting.)

More than 39 million Americans now live below the poverty level—that's more than 15 percent of the population. Who has been hit the hardest? One of every three blacks or Hispanics in America lives in poverty. Almost 15 million children under eighteen live below the poverty line—about 22 percent of all American children.

Half of all black children are already in poverty, and while the number of poor children is growing, that number, according to predictions, will be made much worse by the Republican "welfare reform" proposals. In addition, 37 million Americans still have no health-insurance coverage. All of these figures are *before* the substantial cuts expected in government programs that now keep many people from sinking further down.

All together, there are about 8.4 million families below the poverty line, *more than half of them having a parent who works*! There just are not enough jobs that pay a livable family wage to go around anymore—and the number of good jobs is steadily shrinking. With corporate downsizing, automation, and transformations of computer technology, the loss of work may become the most pressing societal issue in America's future. That is a profound concern for anyone who cares about what is happening to families, but it is not on the agenda of the Christian Coalition.

When 1 percent of the population owns 48 percent of the wealth, where is our sense of community? When the 45 percent of the people on the bottom own only 2 percent of the wealth, what do we mean by democracy? What is the legacy of Martin Luther King's dream when every black child has only a fifty-fifty chance of escaping poverty? And what is the political health of a society when the corporations that financially back congressional candidates are now busily at work, literally in their own corporate suites, rewriting the new federal legislation and environmental regulations that will most affect their companies?

The *Fortune* 500 companies have hardly created a job in two decades due to corporate downsizing, wage reductions, financial mergers, and the paper-shuffling false economy of Wall Street, which creates the "wealth without work" and "commerce without morality" that Gandhi warned against. *Newsweek*'s suggestions that CEOs should show more concern for workers and also take pay cuts when they lay people off are just not enough; and Pat Buchanan's rhetoric of blaming everybody, from immigrants to foreign nations to affirmative-action beneficiaries, is both simplistic and divisive.

The *Newsweek* article took "the hit men" to task for their lack of a community ethic. "It used to be a mark of shame to fire workers en masse. Today Wall Street loves it. But the pants have been scared off the public and stirred a political backlash. Is there a better way?" Yes, there is.

A "Community Economy"

First of all, we need to examine some of our reigning economic assumptions. To recover the idea of the common good, we must reclaim economics as a fundamentally moral and social discipline. Historically, economics rested on the classic tripod of labor, land, and capital.

Human, natural, and financial resources are all vital to economic life, and must relate well to each other for the healthy functioning of an economy and a society. Those relationships are now fundamentally out of balance.

Indeed, economics is about *relationships*—an interdependent web of relationships. Raising one leg of the tripod high above the others causes social or ecological imbalance. That is exactly what has happened as the financial dimension of economic life has achieved a brutal ascendancy over the others, i.e., labor and land. The result is a loss of just social relationships, political fairness, and the connection to the earth.

In economics, as in all of life, individuals are always connected to the community. Economic ideology today falsely polarizes the individual from the community. That separation is illusory and distorts our economic decisions and policies. Any economy must be productive, responsible, and just—three reasonable tests. Those on the traditional Left must accept the test of productivity and fiscal responsibility, while those on the traditional Right must accept the test of just and sustainable relationships.

Laissez-faire capitalism has often failed to adequately account for the needs of the community. While state socialism has collapsed, multinational corporate capitalism has yet to pass the moral tests of equity or ecology. Economics is not just a relationship between persons, but also between individuals and the community, and finally between the human community and the ecological world in which it lives. All those relationships must have integrity. The "common good" requires us to consider them all—people to people, people to community, and species to the environment. The global economy today is a result of the loss of both human community and ecological harmony.

In property transactions, for example, there are several legitimate interests to be considered: the interests of the buyers and sellers, the concerns of the "neighbors," the welfare of the "next generation," and the well-being of "the land" itself. All must be taken into account for the sake of the common good. Indeed, this is what Catholic teaching speaks of as the "social mortgage on property." The environmental question is how the natural resources are to be used, the social question is who gets to use them, and the economic question is who puts what in and takes what out.

Therefore, the false wall between public and private must come down, because both are always involved in economic transactions and relationships. The origins of wealth are always both private and public, and from a religious point of view, all property and economic resources are "on loan" to us as stewards. Ultimate ownership is an important spiritual and political issue; the Psalmist says, "The earth is the Lord's and the fullness thereof."

These are all moral questions that must be asked in

our current economic discussion. Some others include: What is economic sufficiency—how much is enough? Can we continue to endlessly repeat the mantras of promised economic growth, as both Democrats and Republicans do, or can we explore some new visions of a "sustainable economy"? Do not the inherent moral worth of each individual and the requirements of a genuine democracy offer a basic challenge to the enormous discrepancies in wealth between people that the "new economy" is galloping to create? And what is the meaning of our spirituality, in the face of the relentless pressure of a consumer society that is poisoning our hearts as much as our environment?

Now let's get practical. If we really want to reduce the deficit, we should start by eliminating the $90 billion of taxpayers' money lost each year to corporations' tax and spending subsidies ("corporate welfare"). Let's just stop subsidizing the rich at the expense of both the middle class and the poor. Let's also reintroduce the concept of social shame and impose it on those corporate giants who get bigger and bigger by shrinking the wages and jobs of their workers. Instead of admiring the high-stakes gamblers of the casino economy, let's treat them as the socially irresponsible and greedy gamesmen that they are. And if social shame isn't enough, let's begin a public conversation about building in appropriate corporate "accountabilities" as the requirement for doing business in our communities and our country, like plant-closing notifications and other reasonable measures being implemented in some places.

On the other hand, let's reward those community-minded entrepreneurs who do not regard a quarterly profit-and-loss statement as their only bottom line. Business can develop a longer-term perspective, and one that takes the needs of workers, the community, and the environment into account. More and more companies are now seeing the advantages of good worker morale for both safety and productivity, of community trust and involvement for long-term business success, of diversity in the workplace as a stabilizing force for democracy, and of environmental protection for the sake of our quality of life and responsibility to the next generation.

If sacrifices are required, CEOs should share in them by cutting their own salaries and benefits. If prosperity comes to a company, the employees should share in the profits. Where appropriate, more businesses should experiment with worker participation in decision making and even in ownership.

Of particular importance is the prioritizing of community-based economic development. Microenterprises, credit unions, land and housing trusts, and a whole myriad of economic cooperatives are all emerging in many places around the country and need to be dramatically expanded. Experiments like the Grameen Bank in Bangladesh, which successfully lends small amounts of capital to very poor families, have shown the tremendous impact that such alternative economic schemes can have. They can be especially effective in creating jobs and new economic activity in abandoned sectors of the global economy. Similar efforts have sprung up all around the United States. Such locally based community economics has shown the capacity to unite people across both conservative and liberal political lines.

Fundamentally in need of change is the way we treat "the poor" in our economic discussions. The poor must no longer be seen as objects of charity, but as a challenge to more just economic relationships. For example, the poor are not so poor as we think. They do have resources but are always on the wrong end of the *resource flow*. Poor families pay more in rent than middle-class people do for their mortgages, keep their money in banks that won't lend in their neighborhoods, and work land that is always owned by others. The alleviation of poverty will not come about through endless subsidies to the poor, but rather through finding ways of restructuring *our relationships* so that poor people will have the access and opportunity to use their own assets. Responsibility and compassion are false dichotomies that must be replaced with a renewed notion of community.

Beyond the limitations and scope of outmoded capitalist and socialist doctrines lie the unexplored possibilities of a "community economy."

O.J. and the Million Man March

The persistence of racism in the United States and the resurgence of racial polarization are still the most vexing issues of American public life. Sometimes brutally apparent and sometimes cruelly subtle, racism has survived the civil rights movement and the theory of an "integrated" society. America's diversity is still seen by many as our biggest problem, instead of our greatest gift and asset.

Multiculturalism *adds* to community. It broadens the experience, deepens the understanding, and enriches the texture of a nation. It is a benefit, not a barrier, to real community. The interface and blending of diverse cultures has often proven to be a powerful generator of energy that unlocks great creativity in a society. But the white-led political referendums to defeat affirmative action say less about the recognized need to reevaluate old racial remedies than they do about a majority culture still in denial about its deeply held attitudes and expectations of white privilege.

White and black reactions to the O. J. Simpson verdict and the Million Man March have graphically shown how little we really do understand each other. And the growing presence of Latinos and Asian-Americans adds new dimensions and other experiences to the needed conversation on race as this country moves dramatically into a multicultural future.

O. J. Simpson and Louis Farrakhan are as contradictory figures as two people could be. The ex-football running back who vaulted airport furniture as a rent-a-car pitchman had perhaps become the preeminent symbol of smiling black assimilation into white society, while the Nation of Islam's charismatic preacher has been the black community's most notorious symbol of racial divisiveness, mixing his gospel of black dignity and self-determination with a continuous chorus of vitriolic epithets directed at whites, Jews, Catholics, women, homosexuals, and even Christianity. That both became lightning rods for again exposing an America so dramatically divided along racial lines is a revealing irony.

The reaction to the O. J. Simpson verdict—starkly polarized responses along clear racial lines—demonstrated how most whites and blacks still completely misunderstand each other. That a majority black jury would come to "reasonable doubt" about the evidence in the O. J. Simpson murder case is as understandable, in the light of that black experience with America's criminal justice system, as is the majority white reaction that trusted the police and prosecutor's case enough to find O.J. guilty.

In Stalin's Russia it was said that no Russian family was untouched by the terror of the communist dictator's regime. In forty-seven years as a white American, the majority of which have been lived in the black community, I have *never* met a black American who has not been touched personally or in his or her immediate circle of family and friends by racially motivated abuse at the hands of the police and judicial system. The same week the Simpson verdict was announced, a new study was released finding that fully one third of all young black men in America are now in jail, on probation, on parole, or somehow involved with the criminal justice system. In most countries in the world today such statistics would suggest a police state.

For most whites such a situation is so completely beyond their experience that they find it almost impossible to comprehend. The police are still the ones you call when a child or spouse is late coming home. While my mother always told us to look for a policeman if we ever got lost, my black friend Butch's mother told her children to be careful to hide from the Detroit police if ever they couldn't find their way home. Our worlds, even while growing up in the same city, were completely different.

O.J. is a wife-beater, a batterer—apart from the outcome of the trial. And two people were murdered. If O.J. did it, he will not avoid the judgment of God, no matter how many lawyers he can pay. And the anguished faces of many women across the country, as they listened to the verdict, reflected the pain of the four million women who are abused every year by the men in their lives. But white disbelief and dismay at the verdict quickly turned to accusations of "racial solidarity" on the part of black jurors.

The black jubilation over the acquittal, however, was not, for the most part, a celebration of O. J. Simpson, nor was it a ringing proclamation of his innocence, nor did it indicate a lack of sympathy for the victims' families. Rather, it reflected a belief that this case hadn't been proven beyond a reasonable doubt, that it had been tainted by police sloppiness and racial corruption, and that a black man had finally had the resources to beat the system, as whites have done for years. As a black pastor said to me, "Most people I talk to believe that O.J. was guilty *and* that he was framed." When white critics suggest that black jurors were not honest or smart enough to find O.J. guilty they just cause further insult, and neglect the fact that the whole jury, including two whites and one Hispanic, reached a consensus that the prosecution failed to satisfactorily prove its case.

Misunderstanding of black feelings was again evident in the reaction of many white Americans to the Million Man March. In the midst of the Simpson verdict's aftermath, hundreds of thousands of black men came to Washington, D.C., on October 16, 1995, in an awesome demonstration of a commitment—to take personal and communal responsibility for rebuilding the families and fabric of the African-American community. It was, indeed, a spiritual day—of brotherhood, peace, and a determination to reverse and heal the violence, disintegration, and despair that have become the grim reaper in black communities across the land.

What whites must understand is that it was the message and *not* the messenger that the legions of black fathers, sons, and brothers came for. Louis Farrakhan's call for the Million Man March filled a vacuum, enabling a massive response to the deepest internal moral crisis that black America has ever faced. *Somebody* had to call for that response, and Farrakhan stepped into a vacuum. Indeed, the leader of the Black Congressional Caucus honestly admitted on the day of the march that all black elected officials working in concert couldn't have brought so many people together. If the truth be told, black church leaders would have to admit the same thing.

But Louis Farrakhan does not have anything close to the moral caliber or credibility of either Martin Luther King or Malcolm X (whose assassination Farrakhan is alleged by many to have been involved in). The success of the march indicates the readiness of millions of black Americans to hear the call to personal rededication, political self-determination, economic reconstruction, and spiritual renewal. Leadership must now rise up from many quarters in the black community to show the way. It is especially a time for a renewal of leadership in the black church, which is far better situated to mobilize the black community and turn this nation in a new direction than the sectarian and divisive Nation of Islam.

Can We Talk?

After the 1992 riots, following the first Rodney King verdict, I joined a delegation of international church leaders in Los Angeles. We were there to conduct hearings and listen carefully to community groups around the city. Some of us met with Crips and Bloods in Watts, who had just made their first truce. Subsequent meetings led to the national Gang Peace Summit in Kansas City the following year.

Two nights later we had a conversation in a very different kind of community. Simi Valley had been the site of the Rodney King trial, the place where an all-white jury had acquitted the police officers seen brutally beating King on the infamous video. Overnight, this sleepy affluent suburb became famous and widely regarded as a bastion of upper-middle-class white racism. It was a notoriety not welcomed by the citizens of Simi Valley.

Several of our delegation traveled to the embattled suburb one night to participate in a dialogue that had been set up between a black church and a white church in Simi Valley. Yes, despite the public perception, there are black people in Simi Valley, mostly middle-class professionals like most of their neighbors. These two churches, while inhabiting the same community, had never before met or spoken together. The atmosphere was tense, perhaps made more so by the presence of outside "church leaders." Nonetheless a substantial conversation followed.

The pivotal moment in the discussion came when a black mother spoke. "My son is a member of the Los Angeles Police Department," she said, "and I become deeply concerned for his safety when he goes undercover."

Across the room a white woman responded with great sympathy. "I am a mother, too, and I know how you must feel. If my son were a police officer and worked undercover, I'd be frightened to death if he had to work with those gangs."

"No, you don't understand," replied the first woman. "When my son takes off that police uniform, he looks like any other young black man in Los Angeles. I'm not afraid of the gangs, I'm afraid of what white Los Angeles police officers might do to my son." You could see the stunned look on the face of the white mother. It was an absolute shock to her to think that this mother would fear her son's fellow police officers more than gang members. Nothing in her experience had prepared her to hear something like that.

All eyes in the room were on the two women. The white woman was clearly amazed at the story, but she could see that the black mother was telling the truth. To her credit the white woman *believed* the testimony of the black woman. It was the turning point in the conversation. More stories followed. Other black mothers expressed their fears about the safety of their children, especially their sons. African-American businesspeople told stories of being dragged out of their expensive cars, accused of being drug dealers, and spread-eagled across their hoods by white police officers. And then white suburbanites shared their fears about driving through black neighborhoods, of being terrified by the riots, and of feeling quite defensive when the media portrayed Simi Valley as a racist enclave.

Real conversation took place that night. People listened to each other and took their neighbors seriously. Even without great class differences in Simi Valley, the utterly different life experiences across the racial divide were evident to everyone in the room. Many expressed regret that such discussions hadn't occurred before, and were especially embarrassed because they were all Christians. Both sides said how much they valued this opportunity and people from each church were appointed to set up more meetings.

A New Conversation on Race

The day after the Million Man March, bipartisan congressional leadership called upon President Clinton to establish a national commission on race relations. But we've had commissions before and their recommendations have usually been ignored. What's needed now is not a new national commission, but a new national *conversation* on race in America. And that must take place in every local community across the country.

We need more than cultural exchanges between different racial communities; we need very focused, very honest conversations on race between white people and people of color. If we ever hope to dismantle America's destructive racial structures and attitudes, it is critical to understand how racism has impoverished us all. Those structures and attitudes still shape American life and block our greatest potential as a nation. And rather than waiting for the politicians to act, the religious community—along with other community groups—should begin to convene those conversations.

Together, we must climb to the place where our diversity is understood not as America's dilemma but as our greatest national resource. If we can do that, it will also be our best contribution to a world now threatened as much by ethnic conflict as by economic confrontation and environmental catastrophe. While the consequences of not talking now are too great to risk, the rewards of racial justice and reconciliation are too important to miss.

The civil rights era is over, and a new understanding between the races must now be diligently sought. Our experiences of America are vastly different. We must come to respect and understand that difference by *lis-*

tening to each other's experiences, *believing* each other's experiences, and finding new ways of working and living together that affirm our racial pluralism rather than trying to homogenize it. Old solutions must be questioned and new answers must be found that are aimed at dramatically improving the quality of life for marginalized communities, rather than merely repeating the slogans of "the melting pot," which only cover over our social failures. Folksinger Charlie King plays a song that defines *a melting pot* as a place where "those on the bottom get burned and the scum rises to the top!"

Public discussion over affirmative action will be pivotal for America's future. The current call by several conservative politicians for its repeal unfortunately represents a desire to turn back in the struggle for racial justice, rather than to go forward. It is based on the fiction of a color-blind society and a denial of still-present institutional racism in America.

Affirmative action policies have tried to help remedy racism in this country, but after thirty years it *is* time to critically review and reexamine how well those remedies are working. Most black leaders I know, for example, now question the kind of affirmative action that benefits middle-class blacks to the exclusion of poor and working-class whites. But as Bill Clinton rightly stated in his critical speech on the subject, affirmative action should be "mended" rather than "ended."

As many political leaders are realizing, affirmative action is not popular today among white voters. But Jesse Jackson makes a telling point when he reminds us that no important gain for racial justice in American history would have survived a popular vote. He also asks why most Americans support the new South African constitution, which guarantees "minority rights" for the white population there, if they don't support the same principle of protection for minority rights at home in the United States?

It is absolutely clear that continuing efforts are still vitally needed to open up opportunities for people of color and for women in America. Genuine diversity must still be a central goal of American democracy, and will simply not be achieved without concerted and focused action.

However, we must critically examine the attitudes that both liberals and conservatives have brought to the discussions of race and affirmative action. Professor Glenn C. Loury of Boston University is a black conservative who now challenges both sides. "By the end of the 1970s I had become disgusted with the patronizing relativism that white liberals seemed inevitably to bring to questions of race. Wearing their guilt on their sleeves, they were all too ready to 'understand' the shortcomings and inadequacies of blacks." The liberal failure to treat blacks as "moral equals," says Loury, "smacked of racism, and I hated it."

But on the conservative ascendancy on matters of

race, Loury says, "It is now fashionable for conservatives to attribute the catastrophe unfolding in the urban ghettos to some combination of mistaken liberal policies and the deficiencies of inner-city residents themselves." He asks how conservatives can treat with "cool indifference" the circumstances suffered by so many black Americans. "Where is their passion? Where is their moral outrage?" Loury says, "In light of the scale of the tragedy unfolding in cities across the land, the narrowly academic and highly ideological posture of conservative intellectuals—who are in effect saying, 'Too bad about what's happening, but we told you liberals so'—is simply breathtaking." Is it paranoia for a black to wonder whether this posture toward urban problems would be embraced with such confidence among conservatives if those inner-city hellholes were populated by whites?

It is time for both white liberals and conservatives to take stock of their racial attitudes.

The Social Order

When I first heard about *The Bell Curve,* a book by Charles Murray and Richard Herrnstein that preaches black genetic inferiority, I remembered an incident last year at our neighborhood center. A little girl, new to the children's program, was talking to one of our volunteers. She said, "I'm ugly." "No you're not," replied the Sojourners worker. "You are a beautiful child. Why do you say that you're ugly?" The nine-year-old African-American girl replied, "I'm ugly because I'm black." Her self-hatred came from existing in a society that is still pervaded by "the rightness of whiteness." I remember thinking that while this little girl may never read *The Bell Curve,* it would have an impact on her life. It would help reinforce a climate that makes her feel uglier and now stupid.

There was really nothing new in this controversial book that proclaimed the inferiority of African-Americans because of IQ scores, and cited alleged genetic differences between blacks and whites as the primary reason for black disadvantage. Murray's old and shallow arguments and thinly disguised racism were roundly discredited by serious scholars and social critics everywhere. But the book got way too much attention, which was undoubtedly the intention of the right-wing foundations who defended this incendiary bombshell. When racism appears in academic robes instead of hoods and sheets, it somehow is more acceptable and becomes a media phenomenon.

There are always those who choose nature over nurture as the cause of our many social ills. Yet such arguments always fail to take adequate account of the fact that the environment, the community in which we live, is so powerful in shaping our lives. Many of the black poor now live in a virtual war zone.

There is the starkest contrast between the support

systems of family, community, school, and church in which I was nurtured as a white, middle-class child and the horrific conditions endured by the African-American children in whose neighborhood I now reside. To say that such an environment of human destruction is not the central cause of low educational achievement and test scores, et cetera, is so utterly foolish it could only be proposed by those who just don't know the lives of the children whose troubles they have written off to bad genes.

Whom does such thinking hurt? Obviously, those already on the bottom. Whom does it help? Of course, the rich and powerful elites who are already on top. What moral value says that a "cognitive elite" should rule and get the greatest rewards? Bluntly put, we have seen many pseudoscientific justifications for wealth and power staying in the same hands. They are all political treatises against community. We seem always to need one more political and moral argument for forsaking the poor; another ideological rationale for a policy assault against the disenfranchised. We need the presumed intellectual evidence for why "those people" have problems that are mostly their own fault and for which the rest of "us" bear no responsibility.

It is indeed an old story. Into the canyon of our great societal divide ride the right-wing intellectuals, telling us it's meant to be this way, there's nothing we can do about it, so we might just as well stop trying, and each of us should dutifully take up our rightful position in the social order. Hierarchy has always been preferable to community to those already in control. If the poor and racial minorities will only cheerfully accept their lower status based on unchangeable genetics or whatever, the rich and white elites will reluctantly accept their burdens of leadership in the society, in what Mr. Murray incredibly calls a "wise ethnocentrism."

Blaming the oppressed for their oppression is nothing new. It's as old as the Bible, which speaks to the problem directly. People are poor, according to the Bible, when *oppression* is involved. And again, the prophets tell us that a nation's righteousness is determined, not by high IQs, but by how it treats the poorest and most vulnerable in its midst.

Politics in the Image of God

Such arguments are never just "academic," they are a political and even theological vision on behalf of the strong over the weak. As such they are both bad politics and bad "theology." The opposition to such racial diatribes should not come solely from African-Americans and other people of color, who must always again rise to defend themselves. Those who divide us should also face rage from white people who are diligently trying to build community across racial lines in this troubled nation. And the moral outrage to such divisive agendas should especially come from the religious community.

That is because these questions are not really "scientific" as much as they are religious. Racial arguments will be defeated more by theology than by sociology. Only language rooted in the religious proposition of the sacred value of all human life will ultimately triumph over the cultural construction used to divide us. The very concept of a "white race" that melds all Europeans (and even others) together is a myth that must be challenged.

Racism is ultimately a spiritual matter. In fact, there is no such thing as "race" in the eyes of God—in whose image we are all created as equal. Race is rooted neither in biology nor culture. Race is a social construct created by human beings for the purpose of justifying oppression. The issue here is much deeper than "managing diversity" as some corporations now define the task. Enjoying each other's music and restaurants, handling each other's artifacts in a superficial multiculturalism won't be enough.

What America must finally face is an ideology of white supremacy that has profoundly distorted our past and still threatens our future. It is a system of white racial privilege that we must confront, built into the very fabric of the nation. Originally created to justify the enormous profits from slavery, it remains as a means to defend the preferential status many white people still expect in America. But it is an idol, a demon, and an affront to God, who made us all God's children.

Only a theologically rooted discourse will ultimately defeat those forces which would undermine community. If there was any religion left in the Religious Right, we should have heard a denunciation of *The Bell Curve* by the Christian Coalition. But it never came. Principled conservatives like Jack Kemp spoke vigorously against Murray, but the Religious Right was never heard from.

The Christian Coalition and like-minded groups on the Religious Right are painfully silent on the question of race in particular. Racism as an issue is absent from the concerns that dominate their political agenda.

Their "pro-family" platform raises the question of whose families they are advocating for. The Coalition's Contract with the American Family might well have been called Contract with the White Middle-Class Family. The concerns and priorities of poor families, even poor Christian families, are just not there. People of color are mostly absent from the constituency of the Christian Coalition, even though many of their conservative concerns about "values" would find deep resonance within black and Hispanic church communities.

So why is the Christian Coalition so white? Does the fact of their mostly white constituency explain why racism has yet to emerge for them as a real and compelling concern? Or are there even deeper reasons?

Pat Robertson spoke in 1995 to the issue of affirmative action. "There are groups in our society who are extremely able. The Chinese, for example, Asian-Americans, they're extremely able and they always score high and are disproportionately represented in the high levels. Same thing generally with the Jewish people. They are very high achievers. They don't like quotas because it will discriminate against them. If you say, 'Well, you can have five Chinese and two Jews, and so forth, and you've got to have fifteen Hispanics, et cetera,' then all of a sudden those people are denied their opportunities. And they are very intelligent and very vocal in society, and this is one of the reasons you're seeing these decisions, I think. It's unfair to these achieving groups, if you will, to deny them opportunities merely because they are of the wrong ethnic group. They consider it un-American."

In the late 1980s Jerry Falwell visited South Africa at the invitation of the white government in Pretoria and returned to America saying that apartheid wasn't really so bad. Falwell attacked Nelson Mandela as a Marxist and said Nobel Peace Prize winner Bishop Desmond Tutu was "a phony."

In 1988 Pat Robertson told his *700 Club* viewers what he thought about economic sanctions against South African apartheid. "This sanctions movement has no relevance to South Africa. It is one hundred percent domestic American politics. It is transforming the racial problem of America to South Africa without any real concern about South Africa. . . . The whole thing is wrong." In 1992 he said, "I think 'one man, one vote,' just unrestricted democracy [in South Africa], would not be wise. There needs to be some kind of protection for the minority, which the white people represent now." After his own trip to South Africa, Robertson said in 1993, "You know this business about South Africa, I've been to South Africa. I know we don't like apartheid, but the blacks in South Africa, in Soweto, don't have it all that bad. Winnie Mandela lived in a $400,000 house in Soweto." I wondered if Robertson's white hosts showed him any other houses in Soweto.

Just before the 1996 New Hampshire primary Pat Buchanan was asked on a Sunday-morning news show if African-Americans would figure in a Buchanan administration. In an astounding answer the political champion of the Religious Right replied, "I wouldn't rule it out."

Pat Buchanan has become a tremendous embarrassment for the Republican party because he has exposed the strategy that Republicans have followed for more than two decades—pursuing white voters by portraying the Democrats as "the party of civil rights." To say the least, that approach has seriously undermined the quest for a national sense of community around issues of race. The problem is Buchanan is too blunt for many Republicans.

Even more embarrassing is that Pat Buchanan won a majority of Religious Right votes in the early primaries, often by a 2 to 1 margin. Buchanan's strong and often bombastic positions on abortion and gay rights certainly contributed to those wins, but the fact that the Christian Coalition's constituency is almost entirely white didn't hurt either.

During the early primaries, the leaders of the Religious Right were locked in a quandary. They had to decide whether to be faithful to their ideology and support Buchanan's candidacy, or to acknowledge his unelectability and take the more pragmatic route of supporting Bob Dole, and then exact concessions from the Republican nominee and platform. Christian Coalition Director Ralph Reed clearly preferred the latter course. They want to win. Other Religious Right leaders favored the more hard-line Buchanan route, but the pragmatists prevailed and Bob Dole will be eternally grateful for the support of the Christian Coalition's establishment.

However, in the early Republican primaries and caucuses, the Coalition rank and file seemed to have faced no such dilemma. In all those contests, Buchanan walked away with the Religious Right prize—winning a *clear majority* of the Christian Coalition's voters. Even as Dole finally began to trounce his right-wing rival in later primaries (with exit polls showing that most voters believed the television commentator was "too extreme"), Buchanan still got the lion's share of Religious Right votes in states as diverse as Georgia and Massachusetts. During this time, Reed privately told Dole *not* to call Buchanan extreme.

What does it mean that Pat Buchanan emerged as the political champion of the Religious Right? In boasting of the influence he would still have on the Republican platform at the San Diego convention, Buchanan declared, "We've got God on our side." Shouldn't the Christian Coalition have been embarrassed and said so?

The question must be asked, "Would Jesus have voted for Pat Buchanan?" or perhaps an even more telling one, "Would Pat Buchanan vote for Jesus?"

The Christian Right's leaders have said very little about the issue of race, and when they do it sends shudders through the country. One of the worst comments on race that the Religious Right has made came from Pat Robertson on his *700 Club* television show on April 25, 1995. Robertson said, "The term *black* really carries with it a militancy, doesn't it? There is something about it that is hard, that says, 'Man, we're going to get you.'" What in the world was the Christian Coalition president talking about? That is absolutely the wrong kind of signal for a leader of the Religious Right to send. Again, where is the leadership on race?

The religious community should lead the way in engaging the racial divide, because overcoming racism is a theological and spiritual imperative. Racial justice and reconciliation must not be given up on, as the nation sometimes seems ready to do. They are *required* of us by a God who loves all the little children, and a Christ who gave his life to break down the barriers between us. The apostle Peter stated that "God is no respecter of persons," and Martin Luther King, Jr., recognized that this would ultimately be a religious issue: ". . . each individual has certain basic rights that are neither conferred by nor derived from the state. To discover where they come from, it is necessary to move back behind the dim mist of eternity, for they are God given."

Signs of Hope

In contrast to Robertson, Falwell, Buchanan, and most of the Religious Right, there are many hopeful signs among conservative evangelical and Pentecostal groups who are becoming deeply convicted about the issue of racism. The new executive director of the National Association of Evangelicals, Don Argue, has already offered strong and vigorous leadership on the issue of race. Early in his tenure as the NAE's new leader, Argue shocked a January 1995 joint session of the predominantly white NAE leadership and the leaders of the National Black Evangelical Association with a public and dramatic declaration of personal and organizational "repentance" for past white racism.

Kneeling before surprised black evangelical leaders,

the new NAE spokesman confessed the "sin" of racism and humbly asked for their prayers and help in seeking a new day among black and white evangelicals. A whole series of steps have followed to make evangelical colleges and organizations more racially sensitive and inclusive.

On October 17, 1994, in Memphis, Tennessee, black and white Pentecostal leaders from many divided denominations came together after eight decades of racial separation to declare their new desire for unity. After the "Memphis Miracle" even the Southern Baptists, a denomination created by its support of slavery, met in 1995 to also repent of their past defense of slavery and racial discrimination. These are extraordinary and highly significant developments. And they point the way for other groups, religious and nonreligious, to overcome the racial barriers that have for so long made real community impossible.

Family Values

Two 1996 films have caused me much reflection. The first was the very popular *Waiting to Exhale,* featuring an all-star cast that included Whitney Houston, with a top-of-the-charts song and soundtrack. It is the story of one failed personal relationship after another in the lives of a close-knit circle of black professional women. In the end, all they have is one another. It attempts to be funny, moving, and quite profitably entertaining; the box office sales suggest that it succeeded.

I watched the movie with a professional woman, and we both left feeling quite distressed. The values portrayed in *Waiting to Exhale* are at the center of what is wrong with society today. The film is an endless procession of sexual promiscuity, personal irresponsibility, broken promises, and shattered dreams. The women involved are far from innocent victims—everybody is implicated in this painful and tragic picture of human relationships and families coming unraveled.

The first problem in the picture is what happens to the people themselves. Life is just a succession of changing bed partners with no enduring relationships. Trust, commitment, fidelity, stability, security, and real intimacy are all lost in the process. Empty lives result, which don't look very pretty even with the beautiful and scenic backdrop of affluent New Mexico "yuppiedom." In a neighborhood like mine, in the inner-city of Washington, D.C., the playing out of those values amid the stark realities of poverty is brutish and ugly.

The second problem is that there is absolutely no room or safe place for children in the midst of these values. Without home environments that are stable and secure, without an example of positive male and female role models, without parents to teach, by their example, what character, commitment, loyalty, and love really mean, many children will simply fall through the cracks of life. The evidence to support that conclusion is now overwhelming.

The second film I saw is an answer to the first. *Once Upon a Time . . . When We Were Colored* is an absolute delight. This movie, starring Al Freeman, Jr., and Phylicia Rashad, hasn't gotten nearly the same publicity and exposure as *Exhale,* which, perhaps, is part of the problem. Adapted from the book with the same title, the film depicts a black community in the South leading up to the civil rights movement. The picture is of a strong and intact community, whose web of life is woven with strong bonds and extended family structures that nurture and care for everyone—especially the children. While the external threat of white racism is ever-present, the internal life of the black community is vibrant and healthy. The community may be poor, but the quality of life is very rich—far beyond anything known by the hapless and lost souls of *Waiting to Exhale.*

The narrator of the story and the author of the book was born to a teenage girl who wasn't married. His compelling testimony is to being raised, and raised well, by a powerful great-grandfather and great-grandmother, by a loving aunt, by older boys and girls, and by a whole community who regarded him as one of their own. It was a community with "family values." Perhaps the heart of those values was expressed by the boy's great-grandfather, played by Freeman, when he confronted the father of the boy who fathered his granddaughter's child. The boy wanted to take responsibility, but his father bitterly complained that they didn't need another mouth to feed. With searing eyes, Al Freeman, Jr., stared the man in the face and said, "Having nothing is no excuse for not doing right!" The film is a story of people using whatever they had to do right, by each other, by God, and, especially, by the children.

These two films epitomize the choices we have today. One is a continued momentum toward disintegration and chaos in our personal and family relationships. The other is a renewed commitment to reweave the web of family and community that has become so painfully unraveled. But this "family values" question has become very difficult and polarized by both the Religious Right and the cultural Left. To move forward, we must simply refuse the false choices being offered by both sides.

The Left has misdiagnosed the roots of our present social crisis, mostly leaving out the critical dimension of family breakdown as a fundamental component of problems like poverty and violence. For too many leftists, family issues are just the issues of the Religious Right, or simply bourgeois concerns. But the Right has seized upon the family agenda and too often turns it into a mean-spirited crusade against women's rights and homosexuals. Their definitions exclude too many people.

I believe we must rebuild strong and healthy two-parent family systems. We desperately need more families with moms and dads and kids, strong male and female role models in both "nuclear" and extended family systems. It's not a matter of whether that should be "the norm"; it simply *is* the norm in this society and every other one. Even with the honest differences between Christians about what the Bible says about homosexuality, there are not many who question that the biblical norm is heterosexual marriage and family (though the biblical patterns often followed the more extended family systems of the time rather than the smaller nuclear family we know today). The question, rather, is how can that family norm be a healthy one. Right now family breakups, broken promises, marital infidelity, bad parenting, child abuse, male domination, violence against women, and the choosing of material over family values are all combining to make the family norm in America more and more unhealthy. A critical mass of healthy traditional families is absolutely essential to the well-being of any society. That should be clear to us by now. How to make our family norm healthy and whole, must be the first question, especially in neighborhoods where intact families have all but disappeared.

But the second important goal must be the protection and support of those who are not a part of that traditional family pattern. It is simply wrong and stupid to blame gay and lesbian people for the breakdown of the heterosexual family. That breakdown *is* causing a great social crisis that impacts us all, but it is not the fault of homosexuals. It has very little to do with them. Their civil and human rights must also be honored, respected, and defended for a society that is good and healthy. It is a question of both justice and compassion. To be both pro family *and* pro gay civil rights could open up some common ground that might take us forward.

The issue of the legal status of same-sex unions is now causing much controversy. But there are voices calling for a middle way. We don't have to change our longstanding and deeply rooted concept of marriage as being between a man and a woman to, at the same time, make sure that long-term gay partnerships are afforded legitimate legal protections in a pluralistic society.

Do we really want to deny a gay person's right to be at his or her loved one's deathbed in a hospital with "family restrictions"? Do we also want to deny that person a voice in the medical treatment of his or her partner? And do we really want all the worldly possessions of a deceased gay person to revert to the family who rejected them thirty years ago instead of going to their partner of the last twenty years? There are fundamental issues of justice and fairness here that can be resolved without a paradigm shift in our basic definition of marriage.

Similarly, there is no reason to demonize single parents, many of whom have been trying to do the best that they can, and some of whom are doing a very good job of raising their kids (admittedly better than some two-parent families). We shouldn't tell single moms (or dads) and their kids that they are not "real families," when their families are as real to them as anyone else's.

At the same time, the overwhelming social evidence now proves that children from single-parent families are doing much worse, in almost every area, than children from two-parent families. And too many are just being devastated. Single parents should not be attacked; they should be supported. And we can do that without suggesting that single-parent families are as equally desirable a goal as two-parent families.

The controversial and difficult issues of family life are too important to be left alone. There are no alternatives to good family life; indeed, the alternative is chaos and social breakdown.

There is no need to redefine family; our need is to renew family life—where husbands and wives are *mutual* decision makers, where moms and dads are *both* responsible for parenting, where family time is as important as vocational calling and more important than material success, where children are the priority, where everyone can grow and be nurtured, and where no one falls through the cracks. A just and compassionate society will also protect its gay and lesbian citizens. Likewise, most single parents would prefer to have partners, but those who don't must be included in the web of family and community relationships that should protect us all.

After seeing *Waiting to Exhale,* I had a sinking feeling in the pit of my stomach. Is this our future? I wondered. But after I saw *Once Upon a Time . . . When We Were Colored,* I felt some hope again. Those "family values" could shape the kind of future where *everyone* would have a place, and *nobody* would be left behind.

Culture Wars

The grim realities of our own growing polarization were brought home to Americans on April 19, 1995, in Oklahoma City. One hundred and sixty-eight people died because they were in the way of somebody's anger at the government. To use biblical language, the tragedy was "a sign of the times," and points to the breakdown of community.

In the days following Oklahoma City there was an almost automatic tendency in the media and among the public to blame foreign terrorists, and most probably Islamic fundamentalists. The sobering realization that it was a homegrown terrorism that destroyed the Federal Building in Oklahoma City and injured and killed so many people, sent shivers throughout the country. Have we become so divided and angry that executing our neighbors (and their children) becomes a political act? Will our ideological passions, economic dislocations, racial polarization, apocalyptic fears, political scapegoating, and culture wars be too much for the fragile American social fabric?

New tribalisms are replacing notions of the common good. Who we are against has become the rallying cry of politics, instead of what we are for. Demagoguery threatens the spirit of democracy as the dialogues of old town meetings are replaced by the new "dittoheads" of talk radio, and Religious Right polemicists who utter the most virulent language against feminists, homosexuals, liberals, and even presidents. When hate talk becomes the language of politics, violence always results.

Instead of dousing the flames of extremist political talk, the Religious Right has too often just fueled the fire. In response to the Oklahoma City bombing Pat Robertson said on his television show, "You know, here on this program and at CBN we have been strong supporters of law enforcement . . . but since the advent of the head of the Justice Department, Janet Reno, things have gotten out of control. Something is just going on that is very unwholesome in this nation and you look for an explanation of this craziness in Oklahoma City and a lot of it goes right back to what happened with the Branch Davidians, Randy Weaver, and these other people. This is shocking abuse of federal power. It's reminiscent of the Nazis, and something has got to be done."

It cannot be an easy task to deal with cultists like

David Koresh and white supremacists like Randy Weaver, especially when they are loaded to the teeth with arsenals. But even if you believe, as I do, that federal agents abused their authority in both instances, that is no legitimate explanation for the murderous bombing of a federal building full of innocent people.

Pat Robertson, Jerry Falwell, and other Religious Right preachers have often used comparisons to the Nazis when describing "the federal government," "homosexuals," "feminists," "Democrats," "the media," and "liberal America." Pat Robertson says, "Just like what Nazi Germany did to the Jews, so liberal America is now doing to evangelical Christians. It's no different, It's the same thing. It's happening all over again. It's the Democratic Congress, the liberal-biased media, and the homosexuals who want to destroy all Christians."

Of particular concern is Pat Robertson's frequent references to the threat of a coming "new world order," which is also a constant refrain of many of the heavily armed militia groups around the country. The federal government becomes the leading enemy in such rhetoric and Robertson goes so far as to implicate many national political leaders in the frightening new-world-order conspiracies. "A single thread runs from the White House to the State Department to the Council on Foreign Relations to the Trilateral Commission to the secret societies to the extreme New Agers. There must be a new world order. It must eliminate national sovereignty. There must be world government, a world police force, world courts, world banking and currency, and a world elite in charge of it all. To some there must be a complete redistribution of wealth; to others there must be the elimination of Christianity. . . ."

Not only is there a great conspiracy, but both Democratic and Republican presidents have been serving it. In his bizarre book *The New World Order,* Robertson sounds like the Michigan militia when he says, "Indeed, it may be that men of goodwill like Woodrow Wilson, Jimmy Carter, and George Bush, who sincerely want a larger community of nations living at peace in our world, are in reality unknowingly and unwittingly carrying out the mission and mouthing the phrases of a tightly knit cabal whose goal is nothing less than a new world order for the human race under the domination of Lucifer and his followers."

Randall Terry, the leader of Operation Rescue, actually speaks out against tolerance. "I want you to just let a wave of intolerance wash over you. I want you to let a wave of hatred wash over you. Yes, hate is good. . . . We have a biblical duty, we are called by God to conquer this country. We don't want equal time. We don't want pluralism." To say that such talk is unconnected to violence at abortion clinics is simply irresponsible.

The many Christians who are morally opposed to abortion (including myself) must be in the forefront of challenging such rhetoric. And the many people who believe in the necessity of rebuilding strong two-parent families with male and female role models (including myself) must be firm in standing against the hateful caricatures and assaults being leveled at homosexuals by the Religious Right. Similarly, secular liberals must be careful not to stereotype religious people, and especially evangelical Christians, as all hatemongers and fundamentalist bomb-throwers. Even if their response is extreme, the Religious Right did not invent the disrespect and discrimination Christians have too often felt at the hands of very secular educational, political, and media institutions.

Unless these social trends can be reversed, the events of Oklahoma City could be a portent of our future. Systems are breaking down, social isolation and fear are growing, and our angry divisions increasingly define our public life.

A Convergence of Concern

Community among diverse peoples is a very fragile thing, but utterly essential to a democracy. Religious leaders, least of all, should be the ones to shred the fabric of our national community. A democratic society demands a critical minimum of respect, even for those who are your political opponents. And a healthy political community requires the ability to listen to the heartfelt concerns of those who differ with you. Our urgent need for renewing civility in our political discourse will be taken up in the next chapter.

One dialogue that might bring some people together is gathering steam around the country. It is creating a new conversation between those who come from very different places on the political spectrum. On the one hand it draws those who oppose abortion and other "right-to-life" challenges like euthanasia and genetic engineering. On the other hand it draws those opposed to nuclear weapons, capital punishment, poverty, and racism out of a radical "concern for life." Both sides are moving toward more "consistency" in their life-affirming convictions. Many draw upon the language first introduced by Joseph Cardinal Bernardin of Chicago, who called for "a seamless garment" of concern for human life. That "consistent ethic of life" is a challenge to those across the political spectrum to defend human life wherever and however it is threatened. Those involved exhibit a commitment to the equality of women and men, and in fact, many women are leading the way in this convergence of concern.

Around the country both pro-life and pro-choice women have founded "common ground" groups, which explore the commitments that the women share. Their example might be a model for the exploration of common ground on a whole series of issues that now divide us. Many are finding that the political extremes that control the debate on many questions don't really speak for the majority of Americans who, on many issues, find themselves in some yet-to-be-articulated middle ground.

For example, Naomi Wolf, an outspoken pro-choice feminist, is now challenging the pro-choice movement not to minimize the real presence of the unborn child in the moral dilemma of abortion and the "real death" involved in an abortion. A new statement by pro-life leaders released in the spring of 1996 tries to move the pro-life movement beyond endless and fruitless arguments concerning criminalization, to a more persuasive public discourse about the moral and cultural climate that permits such a high abortion rate. Both are significant efforts to move toward more common ground.

The religious community can play a crucial leadership role in rebuilding community by bringing diverse groups to the table, offering the moral force necessary to break down the walls that divide us, and healing the fear and suspicion that now threaten our body politic. A change in our social and cultural values—a spiritual task—is now as important as marshaling the political will and economic resources to build community at the local level.

But it all comes back to our relationships to each other. Oklahoma City shows us how tenuous those relationships have become. Reweaving the fabric of life that holds us together must become our most important political priority. Nurturing the bonds of family and community is as important as creating new jobs. Community-based development will depend upon the formation of better personal and social values as much as on the infusion of necessary resources. It's all connected, as are we.

Who can bring us together? Who will fashion solutions at the local level that really work and don't just satisfy powerful interest groups? Who will treat with equal gravity the signs of cultural breakdown, violent division, and the indicators of systemic social injustice? Who will call for a cease-fire in our cultural wars before they are completely out of control? And who will begin to provide new political leadership in grassroots communities without waiting for Washington to get it right?

Whether Oklahoma City becomes a harbinger of a frightening future or a wake-up call to new possibilities all depends on us.

"God Don't Make No Junk!"

As the sign on the wall of our Sojourners Neighborhood Center says, GOD DON'T MAKE NO JUNK! The slogan is very popular with the kids. And in any religious teaching, individual rights are always seen in the context of promoting the spirit of community. Human dignity will only be recognized and protected in relationship with others. Such a "theology of community" is what our political process most needs today.

Let me illustrate with a personal example from our

little neighborhood center. We run a "freedom school" every day in one of Washington, D.C.'s most violent sections. Children who are at risk from the neighborhood are teamed up with young staffers and volunteers in their early twenties.

Here's what happens. An eight-year-old girl is in a group led by a twenty-year-old student from nearby Howard University. They develop a relationship. After a while the little girl looks at that older college student and says to herself, "She's a black woman, just like I'm going to be. She's smart and in college. She thinks I'm smart and should go to college too. . . . Maybe I will!" Meanwhile, the college sophomore says to herself, "This kid is changing my life! The time I spend with her is the best and most important part of my week. I can't just go back to my studies and career plans as if nothing has happened to me. I want to do something with my life that will make some difference in the lives of kids like her."

There is a transaction going on here. It is not somebody "doing something" for somebody else. Both people are being changed, each is impacting and enlarging the other. They are learning about both relationship and community. And what they are doing, at the deepest level, is contributing to the common good—both of them.

The personal story also has political ramifications. Public policies should be examined on the basis of whether they serve the common good, or whether they simply are advancing some special interest. Like our rule of thumb regarding compassion, the voices calling us to community are often the ones that are speaking for God.

It is only a healthy sense of community that makes for a healthy political society. Conversely, when the gaps between us become too large, because of race and ethnicity, economics and class, gender, generational difference, or whatever else, it bodes ill for the body politic. Democracy, in fact, depends upon a healthy sense of solidarity and common purpose among citizens.

To find a new sense of community is now America's most important political task. It will not be easy, but the only thing more risky is to move into America's pluralistic future without any real understanding of one another. It's time to go forward.

FOUR

Civility: The Third Test of Politics

"It is interesting that termites don't build things, and the great builders of our nation almost to a man have been Christians, because Christians have a desire to build something. He is motivated by a love of man and God, so he builds. The people who have come into these institutions are primarily termites. They are destroying the institutions that have been built by Christians, whether it is universities, governments, or our traditions that we have . . . the termites are in charge now, and that is not the way it ought to be, and the time has arrived for a godly fumigation."

—Pat Robertson, *The 700 Club*

I had just flown across the country from Seattle to Boston's Logan Airport. It was the fall of 1994 and we were right in the middle of one of the nastiest political campaigns in most people's memory. It was also the middle of the night and I was very tired, but the cabdriver who picked me up was very talkative. "So why are you in Boston?" he wanted to know. Sleepy eyed, I told him I was on a book tour. His interest was piqued. "What's the name of your book?" When I answered, he became very pensive. *"The Soul of Politics.* . . . I'll need a little time to digest that. . . . I didn't think politics had a soul. But it's supposed to, isn't it?"

"We don't have leaders anymore," said the cabdriver, "just politicians." I asked him who he thought some real political leaders might be. "That Gandhi fella," he said, "—now, he was a leader." So, in Boston's wee morning hours, we had a long taxicab discussion about the leadership of Mohandas K. Gandhi.

I told him what Gandhi once said about the moral temptations of political power. In the midst of his fight for India's independence, Gandhi remarked, "My first fight is with the demons inside of me, my second fight is with the demons in my people, and only my third fight is with the British." There were times, in India's long march to freedom, that Gandhi would actually call off the movement for years at a time, much to the frustration of his colleagues in the Congress party. The great Mahatma would say that they weren't ready for freedom yet and that more work on social, economic, and spiritual development was necessary, often including periods of fasting.

My companion and I both commented on how rare it is to find that kind of moral introspection in political leaders today. The cabdriver's response to a "soulless" politics in America today typifies that of many people I meet as I travel across the country. Two strong themes emerge. First, people from many walks of life and across the political spectrum are deeply hungry for an alternative political vision with real moral values—many would say spiritual or even religious values. But second, many people are afraid of the Religious Right.

The Importance of Civility

If you ask people what they find most offensive about politics today, they will often cite the bitter rhetoric and "attack" campaigns of modern political warfare. "All they do is shout back and forth and call each other names," said one disgusted citizen after an early-1996 primary debate. Gandhi's self-examination and political introspection contrasts dramatically with our Democratic and Republican partisans today. Across the political spectrum we suffer from a *loss of civility*.

"Civility" is really about two things: the quality and integrity of our public discourse, and the level and depth of citizen participation in the political process. The two are deeply connected.

Politics has always been tough, but the nature of political discussion seems to have reached a new low across America—in the halls of Congress, on the campaign trail, in local communities, and even in the churches! Many veteran political observers are commenting that what we now experience is substantially different from the "rough and tumble" of politics as we have often known it in the past.

The public square has been poisoned by a *fundamental disrespect* in the political debate. And the political process itself has become more and more closed to genuine citizen democracy.

Being so disrespectful in our political discussion does something to the body politic. Treating opponents and opposing ideas with contempt has consequences that affect us all. It poisons the debate, polarizes the options, and prevents us from finding real solutions to our many problems.

Public discussion *should* be vigorous, sharp, and competitive. All of our often competing interests, values, and constituency needs must be brought to the table for democracy to remain healthy. But disrespect is a different thing altogether.

The lack of civility actually hurts people and damages the democratic process. To put it spiritually, much of our political discourse today dishonors the image of God in each other and in the fragile process of human beings trying to govern themselves in peace. The final line of the Pledge of Allegiance stands as the sharpest rebuke to most of our strident political rhetoric today: "One nation under God, indivisible, with liberty and justice for all."

The lack of civility makes it almost impossible to find common ground. A political search to find answers to serious problems has been replaced by the politics of warring factions, where winning and losing become the only considerations. We must do more than simply change our language; we must learn to *honor* the process and its participants by treating disagreement with respect.

When political discourse is so "uncivil," it *discourages* citizen involvement. If politics is characterized mostly by blaming and scapegoating, it creates public cynicism and withdrawal. Every issue that affects the level and the quality of citizen participation in politics is an issue of civility. For example, the dramatically increased power of money over the political process—in the back rooms of Congress or in campaigns of people whose personal fortunes allow them to outspend all their competitors—is a challenge to political civility because it blocks the access and influence of ordinary people in the decisions that govern their lives.

Today few people believe you can get to the top of the political heap without being corrupted, and that is a dangerous development. Honesty, respect, principle, openness, fairness, accessibility, and involvement are all issues of civility. In the democratic clash of values there must be some agreement about the values of the public discourse itself. The ways we disagree can sometimes be as important as the things upon which we agree.

Can we differ strongly with our opponents and still value the worth and human dignity of our adversaries?

Can we energetically seek to influence public policy and remain committed to the fairness of the political process? Do we ultimately believe in the value of a pluralistic democracy? Can the Religious Right agree to these values? Can the liberal Left? Can the Republicans and Democrats?

Citizenship is about honoring the political process by becoming involved in it. But for citizens to want to participate, they must *believe* in the integrity of the process. (Or that it can be made more fair.) In other words, they must believe it is possible to make a difference. Otherwise, why try? The widespread feeling among many Americans that their vote and involvement won't make a difference anymore is an alarming situation. It is a crisis of civility.

The real issues in our public life today have much more to do with "values" than ideology. Underneath the surface of political discussion there is a crisis of values. The false cultural values of materialism, greed, violence, promiscuity, and selfishness, for example, have an enormous impact upon our public life but are seldom discussed as political issues. The politics of the future will draw its moral heart from a renewal of more positive values rather than from agendas of special interest groups. A public discussion of values must replace ideological confrontation.

The issues that ravage our cultural and political debate are exacerbated by the now dysfunctional categories of liberal or conservative, Left or Right. While those ideological paradigms still rule in the political parties, the media, and in the debates of Congress, they just don't work anymore on the street and in local communities, where people are looking for practical solutions to real and painful problems. We are paralyzed by the politics of false choices and we need a fundamentally new approach.

The Search for a New Approach

President Franklin Roosevelt is lauded by a broad spectrum of American politicians, from modern-day Democrats to Ronald Reagan and Newt Gingrich. On the fiftieth anniversary of his death journalist David Brinkley commented that before Roosevelt, the hungry were just told to go to a church, charity, or soup line. Roosevelt introduced a new notion of social and public responsibility, which has since been widely accepted. Now many question the role of government in solving social problems. But those who say that the answer is to go back to a total reliance on religious and private charity miss the point.

Government is neither the only nor, sometimes, the best mechanism by which a nation exercises its social responsibility. But, as a *society,* we are responsible for one another. Taking social responsibility is a moral and religious imperative that cannot always be shifted to someone else.

Indeed, this is *the* inherent problem of the welfare state: we have come to depend too much upon the federal government for solving problems that local communities are often better situated to take on. But neither can we leave those problems to be solved by the private sector alone. The battle ahead is for an entirely different approach by which we might reverse the downward spiral of our nation: underclass poverty and middle-class insecurity, moral breakdown, social polarization, and growing violence.

The good news is that people across the country are hungry for new visions and approaches—and the honest political leadership required to find them. Three things will be required to achieve them. First, there must be a recognition that neither the state nor the market can solve the problems we now face. As we have already discussed, the role of the "civil society," through the institutions of family, school, neighborhood, voluntary associations, churches, synagogues, et cetera, will be critical.

Second, while government cannot solve all of our social problems and is ill suited to address many of them, the public sector must still play a crucial role. The wall between public and private solutions must be broken down in favor of new "partnerships" and configurations of people and resources in local communities working together. What a catalytic public leadership role might be and how such new partnerships in local communities can be convened should be a central focus of political conversation.

Political columnist E. J. Dionne believes the current political upheaval should be seen as "less a revolt against *big* government than as a rebellion against *bad* government—government that has proven ineffectual in grappling with the political, economic, and moral crises that have shaken the country." In his book *They Only Look Dead,* he predicts the growing influence of "progressives" who take moral and spiritual values seriously. "The Progressive goal is not to strengthen government for government's sake, but to use government where possible to strengthen the institutions of civil society." The purpose of good government, he says, then, should be "to strengthen nongovernmental institutions."

Third, without new moral energy, along with the resources (both human and financial) adequate to the scope of the task, the job will not get done. That pleads for the involvement of the churches and religious community. The business community must play its part as well, and follow the lead of those innovative entrepreneurs who now include both the common good and environmental responsibility as part of their bottom line. Marian Wright Edelman, of the Children's Defense Fund, is prophetic when she challenges us to "leave no child behind." Our children are the moral imperative that must become "the measure of our success."

We need a politics of community and a politics of hope that can begin to bring us together. Given the wars of Washington, that kind of politics will most likely emerge first in local communities led by citizens with a moral vision of social transformation. It is a battle not well left to the politicians but one that calls for nothing less than the spiritual renewal of our practice of citizenship.

Moral Values

I was speaking in New York City to a group of foundation executives, who were all liberal funders of artistic and social causes around the country. Their immediate concerns, which I was asked to address, included the "culture wars," the Religious Right, and the Republican takeover of the Congress. After I spoke, several people in the audience jumped down my throat. "We will not sell out to racism, homophobia, and right-wing politics," they declared. I was puzzled. Having never been accused before of even being a "moderate" on issues like racism, I asked what I had said to have led to such an outburst. "You used the phrase *moral values,*" one of them replied. "And what do those words mean to you?" I asked. "They mean 'right wing'!" agreed my accusers. I responded, "If the liberal Left concedes the whole territory of public discourse over moral values to the Religious Right, you will lose the cultural and political wars. And, indeed, you will deserve to lose."

Most Americans believe that we have suffered a decline in moral and religious values in this country. And they are right. The failure of liberals, the Left, progressive movements, and the Democratic party to connect with that concern is the principal reason for the rise of the Right. The Right taps into people's longing for a society more respectful of traditional notions of right and wrong, of "family values," and of personal responsibility. In conceding the public conversation of such matters to the zealots of the Republican and Christian Right, progressives have made a costly mistake.

It has allowed terms like *family values* to be turned into a kind of code language that would push women back into old patriarchal molds, defend old hierarchies of race and class, and scapegoat gay and lesbian people as if homosexuals are the ones responsible for the disintegration of the traditional two-parent family. The mom, dad, and kids family is in real trouble in America (and that, as we have said, is a very serious problem); but it's not because of homosexuals being guaranteed their basic human rights. To prove one's commitment to family values with hateful rhetoric against homosexuals is just plain wrong.

In taking over the language of "values," the far Right has used the opportunity to impose an utterly reactionary political and economic agenda that has nothing to do with moral, and especially religious, values. (Intolerance, self-righteousness, sectarianism, social divisions, and class distinctions are not among our best religious principles.) We now see many Americans who are so hungry for the cultural values they hold dear, that they vote for a right-wing agenda that runs counter to their own real interests.

Some even suspect that the Right's economic and political agenda has always been more important to them than the social and cultural issues around which they publicly mobilize their constituencies. Are tax cuts for the rich, freeing corporations from environmental regulations, dismantling public aid to the poor, and ending affirmative action ultimately more a priority to the Right than the protection of unborn lives and the integrity of the family? It's a fair question.

Several weeks after my exchange with the foundation heads in New York, I was back in the same conference room speaking to a group of activists from progressive political organizations. They were also gathered to assess the meaning of the Republican political takeover. The letter of invitation boldly suggested that in light of the massive conservative electoral victory, progressive movements needed to reconsider their entire political agenda, "including the dimension of spirituality." The meeting was a real breakthrough. I was one of only two representatives from the religious community present, but the lively discussion of how a progressive economic and political vision must be rooted in the solid ground of moral values and our best religious traditions was a refreshing balm to the soul.

Economic justice and social equality are political principles, but they are deeply rooted in the religious assertion of our common identity as children created in the image of God. Our interconnectedness is the reason why we must reweave the web of families and communities that has suffered such unraveling. And that very sense of community requires a renewed sense of *both* personal and social responsibility to restore a vision of the "common good" in all of our neighborhoods around the country.

Most Americans want a "civil society" characterized by the values of integrity, honesty, responsibility, fairness, openness, and, above all, genuine citizen involvement. That popular involvement is indeed key. *Civility* means more than the quality of our public discourse, it requires the participation of the citizenry in shaping the political direction of the country.

Beyond Liberal and Conservative

There is an alarming depth of cynicism in every region of the country toward politics as usual. People are literally sick of politics defined by image, style, hype, spin, money, power, and, most of all, attack. But there is also a palpable hunger for a politics of vision, values, integrity and credible leadership, and a longing to recover the moral heart of our public debate and the "soul of politics."

Most Americans believe that politics is simply not working, especially at the federal level. Many just do not sense that their government is responding to either the moral *or* the economic crises that they feel. Nor is politics speaking to either their values or their anxieties. We are facing, at the same time, both social disintegration and political dysfunction, and that is a dangerous combination.

Today, people want answers more than ideology. The old solutions of the Left and the Right, and the bitter conflict between liberals and conservatives, seem increasingly irrelevant and distasteful to people in their own communities. Many people care both about the moral values that have concerned the conservatives *and* the issues of justice and equity that have preoccupied the liberal agenda. As a Republican mayor wrote to me recently, "We need the moral values the conservatives care about, and the social conscience of the Left."

For too long liberals and conservatives have been talking past each other. Anyone who lives in a neighborhood like the one in which our inner-city congregation works knows too well how irrelevant and dysfunctional the liberal and conservative categories have become. Each tends to dwell on some aspects of our social crisis and ignore the others. The truth is that we need to recover both the language of personal moral values and a passion for social justice.

Conservatives nobly stress individual virtue and responsibility, but then forget how real racism still is in American society and how poverty is enforced and perpetuated by unjust social and economic structures. Liberals are right to speak of society's responsibility for the disenfranchised, but they have relied too much on governmental solutions to problems that can only be solved by other means—like reweaving the fabric of family life, restoring the spirit and bonds of local communities, and remaking the social covenant that has broken down between polarized groups.

Neither liberal nor conservative agendas are empowering the poor, creating community, or building bridges between our society's warring factions. Neither big government nor big corporations can be relied upon to serve the common good. And neither endless public subsidies nor alleged trickle-down economics will generate real and lasting solutions to endemic social injustice and the collapse of cultural values. In contrast, it will be community-based strategies which combine personal responsibility, family, work, and social justice that now have the best chance of success.

In the end it comes down to a question of values. What are our values? What kind of people and country do we want to be? What sort of political process can find solutions to the vexing problems of our common life? What kind of world are we leaving to our children? And what do we really mean by *democracy*?

In a variety of local communities diverse people and groups are beginning to come together seeking a politics with spiritual values that transcends the old options of Left and Right. Religious and nonreligious alike, pastors and teachers, neighborhood organizers and parents, mayors and former gang members, are forging new relationships around needed moral visions that take seriously both personal and social transformation.

The religious community can play a crucial leadership role in getting other groups to the table and offering the necessary moral vision needed to confront the depth of the crisis we now endure. A change in our social and cultural values is now as important as marshaling the economic resources and political will to rebuild our disintegrating communities. And that will be a spiritual task.

A Lack of Civility

Our current "cultural wars" and political polarization have served to *decrease* real citizen involvement in politics and, at the end of 1995, literally led to two shutdowns of the government. It was an extraordinary spectacle. The ideological impasse over the national budget debate virtually stopped the wheels of government from turning for weeks at a time. Most people around the country seemed either indifferent or irritated, or both. When the Republicans and Democrats finally agreed to compromises that would reopen the government temporarily, the largest East Coast snowstorm in seventy years shut down the government completely. It was as if God were offering an opinion on the "uncivil" paralysis and polarization of American politics.

During the House of Representatives debate on welfare reform, a millionaire Republican congressman from Florida compared poor people to the "alligators" in his state—if you feed them, you make them dependent. That inspired a Wyoming GOP congresswoman to make the same point about wolves in her Rocky Mountains. On the other side some Democratic voices compared those who supported block grants to the states to Nazis. One congressman lamented it was the worst debate in all his years on Capitol Hill. "We are pulling apart in this country," he said.

Alongside the repeated government shutdowns and bombastic political rhetoric, a record number of politicians, from both parties, decided to retire. It had been one hundred years since so many congressional officeholders had left at the same time. Most of those who have burned out on political service are the moderates from each of the political parties. Washington has just become too "mean" for them, too polarized, too ideological, and too money-focused. Fund-raising takes more of their time than innovative political thinking, and they all say that entrenched ideological warfare has replaced the bipartisan search for real solutions.

In a *Nightline* program both Republican and Democratic congressional retirees testified as to why they had lost heart. They said the political extremes now control the political debate. The far Left and the far Right dictate political strategy while most Americans are somewhere in the middle. And the media especially was held culpable. The political self-exiles echoed a bipartisan complaint that the media is "more interested in conflict than with clarity." The media managers think they are "fight promoters," said one retiring congressperson.

One member of Congress recently told me, "Some of us up here are desperate for new ideas." Many Americans are looking for new ideas too. A *Newsweek* cover story, in September of 1995, proclaimed a "radical middle" in the American electorate between the polarized extremes; and the widespread public interest in potential third-party candidates—from Ross Perot, to Bill Bradley, to Colin Powell—suggests the desire for political change, even beyond the merits of the candidates themselves. A new grouping of former governors, senators, and congresspersons from both parties have now come together calling for a "sensible center" of fiscal responsibility, social compassion, and campaign finance reform. New political language of "common ground" and even "higher ground" could rejuvenate public interest in politics—*if* a commensurate vision is forthcoming.

The Religious Right

The Religious Right has become notorious for its lack of civility. The discourse of politics has become the language of war when Ralph Reed talks about "taking back this country, one precinct at a time," and Pat Buchanan says they will do it "block by block," if necessary. Pat Robertson compares non-Christians to termites "destroying institutions that have been built up by Christians," and tells his followers to "expect confrontations that will not only be unpleasant but at times physically bloody." Reed uttered the now infamous quote describing his strategy as the executive director of the Christian Coalition: "It's better to move quietly, with stealth, under the cover of night. . . . I want to be invisible. I do guerrilla warfare. I paint my face and travel at night. You don't know it's over until you're in a body bag. You don't know until election night." Since then he has counseled his political troops to replace "military metaphors" with "sports metaphors."

Is this the proper role for religion in our political debate? In the midst of ideological warfare it is up to the religious community to sort out the real moral issues at stake and bring people together around common concerns. And when religious conviction calls for principled and even unpopular stances, shouldn't the way those opinions are expressed exemplify the kind of moral discourse that ennobles a political society, rather than dragging it deeper into the mud? Isn't how we treat our opponents as important, religiously, as the moral principles we stand for?

In a politically volatile environment, *signals* from the national level are very important, both positive and negative. Both good leadership and bad leadership make a great deal of difference—whether from the political or the religious world.

The Religious Right is guilty of one of the worst sins of politics: the denigration of "the other." In facing a complex dilemma it is always easier to look for someone to fear or blame than it is to find practical solutions. But fear and blame have become the primary political tactics of the Religious Right. Their relentless attacks on their political opponents regularly employ caricature, exaggeration, distortion, hysteria, and character assassination.

They seldom stick to the issues and debate them fairly. Rather, they consistently resort to assaulting the honesty, integrity, decency, patriotism, faith, and even the humanity of their enemies. In so doing the Religious Right has modeled a politics that both defies and disdains civility.

In addition to the already cited aspersions cast against the poor, people on welfare, and blacks, targets of the Religious Right include women, feminists, pro-choice advocates, liberals, liberal Jews, Democrats, the federal government, the media, gun-control advocates, legal-services lawyers, public-school teachers, other religions and even mainline church denominations, and homosexuals, who are singled out for the most vitriolic attacks.

The lack of civility by the Religious Right took on new dimensions with their political champion, Pat Buchanan. His outspoken views and blame-mongering against many kinds of people suddenly got national attention. Two days after Buchanan's win in New Hampshire *USA Today* treated the country to some of those opinions, such as, "If we had to take a million immigrants in, say, Zulus, next year, or Englishmen, and put them in Virginia, what group would be easier to assimilate?"

Christian Coalition President Pat Robertson's most famous quote about feminists came in a fund-raising letter against an Equal Rights Amendment in Iowa: "The feminist agenda is not about equal rights for women. It is about a socialist, antifamily political movement that encourages women to leave their husbands, kill their children, practice witchcraft, destroy capitalism, and become lesbians." The television preacher's views on women are motivated by a patriarchal theology of the family, which he believes should structure the social order as well. "God intended men to be the high priest of their families. They are to be in touch with God and to be the one who's the spiritual head. There is such a thing as headship. And I don't care how much the feminists scream about it, the Bible says that Jesus is the head of the man, and the man, in turn, is head of the family and the head of the wife."

Both Pat Robertson and Pat Buchanan have doubts about the ability of women to be equal to men. Buchanan says, "Rail as they will about 'discrimination,' women are simply not endowed by nature with the same measures of single-minded ambition and the will to succeed in the fiercely competitive world of Western capitalism." Robertson says, "There's a difference from birth. Now, the male mind thinks in certain attitudes. . . . But the key in terms of mental—it has nothing to do with physical—is chess. There's never been a woman grandmaster chess player. And if, you know, once you get one, then I'll buy some of the feminism, but not until that point."

Robertson comes down particularly hard on working women. One can easily surmise the reasons why. Working women represent a threat to his ideal of the patriarchal family. On working women, Robertson comments, "From everything I can gather, by the time a woman gets through paying cosmetics, lunch, transportation, baby-sitters, all the rest of it plus taxes, maybe she nets nineteen hundred to two thousand dollars a year. Let it go and take care of those kids. I mean, that's the thing to do. Restructure the way you live and boost your husband so he will feel support and maybe he can get a raise."

Singled out for particular blame in America's problems are the liberals to support Robertson's own ideological bias that conservatives have all the answers and liberals have none. "They've got no business being in charge of a country that was founded by godly people," says Pat Robertson. "It's time Christians got mad and said, 'We've had enough of this. We want our nation back, in a sense. We want our rights and privileges back. We want our symbols back and our beliefs back.' " In fact, when Robertson says we need more religious values and people in public life, he really means exclusively Religious Right people and values. It is simply assumed in the Christian Right that political liberals couldn't possibly be religious people: "The hatred of God in our society among the so-called liberals is extraordinary. This religious cleansing has just reached fever proportions," Robertson exclaims. When asked on one occasion about the Christians in other Protestant denominations, he replied, "You say, 'You're supposed to be nice to the Episcopalians and the Presbyterians and the Methodists and this, that, and the other thing.' Nonsense. I don't have to be nice to the spirit of the Anti-Christ."

Pat Robertson, who is still the president of the Christian Coalition, flat out says that he has a religious test for public office in this country. He says those who hold governmental authority in the country should be either "Christians or Jews." When asked if he was saying that there are no other people qualified to be in government besides Christians and Jews, Robertson replied, "Yeah, I'm saying that I think anybody whose mind and heart is not controlled by God Almighty is not qualified in the ultimate to be the judge of someone else and I think judges should be in turn submitting to the judge of the universe."

Despite a more mixed history in which the U.S. was founded by a combination of Deists and humanists, as well as Christians, Robertson again and again ties the American form of government to biblical Christianity almost exclusively. Jesus Christ "came to give us a Christian country," Robertson has said. "Our form of government comes directly from the Bible," and that's why "the time has come for God's people to be where He intended them, on top, not on the bottom." He firmly believes, "This is a Christian nation." As such the Christians should rule. "I think Christians were intended by God to be the leaders." And that means taking charge. "God's plan, ladies and gentlemen, is for His people to take dominion. . . . What is dominion? Dominion is lordship. He wants His people to rule and reign with Him."

Jerry Falwell has put out titillating videos suggesting that President Clinton is a sexual pervert and might even be guilty of murder in Arkansas. Robertson says, "You don't expect the president to be a sleazy liar," and has suggested that the Vincent Foster tragedy "was not suicide. It looks more and more like murder now." Disagreement with President Clinton is perfectly reasonable on the part of the Religious Right, but there have never been such hateful diatribes directed at the White House from religious leaders as in the past four years. Hillary Clinton has been especially vilified by groups on the Religious Right. "God and morality," says Robertson, "the Clinton administration wants out of the country."

But the most venomous attacks from the Religious Right are regularly directed at homosexuals, as they play upon people's fears that gays are "going to take your children and your grandchildren and turn them into homosexuals" (says Robertson). Sometimes conservative Christians complain that their sincerely held theological convictions against the practice of homosexuality are termed "homophobic." That's a fair complaint. But even Christians who believe their biblical faith does not support homosexuality can refrain from the hate talk against homosexuals. Indeed, many do and, support basic civil rights for gays and lesbians. Evangelical leader Tony Campolo and several Catholic bishops are good examples of religious conservatives who nonetheless preach against homophobia and defend the human rights of their gay brothers and sisters.

But Pat Robertson says, "[Homosexuals] want to

come into churches and disrupt church services and throw blood all around and try to give people AIDS and spit in the faces of ministers. . . ." He says, "When lawlessness is abroad in the land, the same thing will happen here that happened in Nazi Germany. Many of those people involved were Satanists. Many of them were homosexuals. The two things seem to go together." Actually, homosexuals were among those who were sent with the Jews to Hitler's concentration camps and ovens.

Especially venal is the practice of many Religious Right groups who use hate and fear of homosexuals as a prime tactic in their fund-raising letters. While not as visible a public figure as he used to be, Jerry Falwell has always used such tactics. He once asked for money, complaining about administration plans to allow HIV-positive people to enter the U.S. for the Gay Games. It wasn't too different from allowing Magic Johnson to play basketball again.

But Falwell said, "Without your donation, there will be scores of angry, hateful, and militant homosexual activists—WHO ARE ALL INFECTED WITH HIV AND AIDS AND OTHER FILTHY SEXUAL DIS-EASES—crossing our borders by the hundreds and thousands. And what will happen when they get here? Well, I'll tell you what will happen. Some of them will leave—but only AFTER they have infected countless other Americans with AIDS and HIV. Others will stay to try to steal drugs and get medical treatment that is *paid for by your tax dollars*. More will hide out in big cities and small towns and spread their perversions in underground sex clubs and smut houses. And then there will be even more of these angry, evil, and misguided homosexual activists who will try to *recruit your children; invade your hometown; put on perverted parades; attack your church; and defame your pastor.*" (Emphases are Falwell's.)

I witnessed the largest gay and lesbian march ever in Washington in 1994. The vast majority of the gay marchers looked like very mainstream middle-class Americans, many even in military uniforms. But in the middle of the parade came the militant activists of the group ACT UP. They seemed determined to shock and offend with the most flamboyant and lewd behavior. Gay men were waving big rubber penises, while lesbian women marched bare breasted. Very sexual chants and slogans loudly announced that ACT UP was here.

Just down Pennsylvania Avenue the fundamentalists were waiting, holding signs that screamed FAGGOTS DIE, and QUEERS GO TO HELL. As the two groups approached each other, tensions rose and the police moved quickly in between. A brawl broke out, all the press cameras took pictures, but eventually everyone moved on. What became most interesting to me was the fund-raising letters from the two sides in the succeeding months. Each used the other as a frightening example of the greatest threat to our liberty and decency. I finally realized that groups like ACT UP and the Religious Right have a symbiotic relationship. They actually need each other— at least politically, and for fund-raising purposes.

The experience taught me a lot about the function of political extremes in our society. Vocal minorities take the media microphones and drown out the silent middle. Civility is the first casualty, and citizen participation is the second. Most people just get disgusted and walk away.

The Religious Right has helped to create a media frenzy over the questions of politics and religion. Bill Clinton gets angry at Jerry Falwell's outrageous attacks, the Democrats raise the specter of the sinister Religious Right wanting to take over the country, and the Republicans claim there is a liberal and media assault going on against all Christians and their values—"Christian phobia," House Speaker Newt Gingrich calls it.

William Bennett complains that the Christian Right has come under unfair attack from liberal Democrats and the media. But attack, after all, has become a principal political weapon of the Religious Right's chief spokespersons. The television preachers are hardly innocent victims of liberal attacks, as they sometimes claim to be. "Mudslingers," Bill Bennett rightly points out, do indeed pollute the political process. But let's all be fair. These days much of our polarizing political talk comes from the Religious Right as well as the liberal Left.

Religion and Politics

Most Americans want a society rooted in moral and religious values. But they don't want a theocracy, a nation "governed by Christians and Christian values" as Ralph Reed has called for, or ruled by the Christian Right's interpretation of "biblical morality," as Pat Robertson puts it. And most Americans think the separation of church and state is a good thing, not a "lie of the left," and an import from "the Soviet Constitution," as Robertson has ludicrously claimed.

The separation between church and state envisioned by the Founding Fathers, as historian Garry Wills points out, was designed to *increase* the influence of religion in public life, not to decrease it. Independent faith, freed from the shackles of state power, would be more able to shape the moral climate and direction of the nation than an established religion dependent upon political coercion.

Constitutional law professor Stephen Carter has rightly argued that the separation of church and state was meant to prevent the intrusion of the state into religion or the imposition of a state religion, and not to restrict the influence of religion in the public square. On the contrary, in America, more than any other nation in the world, religious conviction has fostered social progress.

Journalist Bill Moyers says he, too, is a Baptist like Pat Robertson, Jesse Helms, Newt Gingrich—and also like Jesse Jackson, Al Gore, and Bill Clinton. He traces his Baptist roots back to Roger Williams, the dissenter who was banished by the Puritans of the Massachusetts Bay Colony for denying their authority over his conscience. The Religious Right seems happier with the theocratic and repressive vision of Puritan leader John Winthrop's "city on a hill," in which, Moyers points out, the Puritans were "king of the hill." That apparently is what the Christian Coalition wants to be too.

Says Moyers of the Religious Right, "They invoke it [separation of church and state] to protect themselves against encroachment from others, but denounce it when it protects others from them. . . . They deplore the coercive power of the state, except when they would use those very powers to force others to do 'the right and moral thing' as they define it. They stand foursquare behind the First Amendment when they exercise their right to criticize others—sometimes with a vengeance and often with vitriol, as when Jerry Falwell circulated videos implicating the President of the United States in murder—but when they in turn are challenged or criticized, they whine and complain that they are being attacked as 'people of faith'. . . . They want it both ways. In the pursuit of power they take no prisoners and give no quarter. But confronted and contradicted, they take refuge in piety and self-pity. They control the Republican party, the House of Representatives, and the Senate, yet from *no* corridor of power in their grasp comes the faintest sound of Christian love or mercy, nor a single refrain of healing."

If religious values are to enter the public square, and I believe they should, the first thing they ought to do is improve the quality and integrity of our political discourse. To begin to do that would require making the current discussion on religion and politics more inclusive. The dialogue must be widened beyond its present limitations by enlarging the table of conversation. As Stephen Carter has pointed out in *The Culture of Disbelief*, there is a fear of religious conviction in the corridors of political power. But in the Christian Right there is a fear of any religiously rooted politics that doesn't conform to their agenda.

The Question of Power

But there are even deeper questions here, and some of them are theological. A better theological discussion of political power than the Religious Right has yet offered might help us find the path to a more civil and democratic future.

The government is frequently attacked these days—political power has become too concentrated, centralized, intrusive, and unaccountable, especially at the federal level. The large and distant bureaucracies that have come to represent the essence of government are regarded with disdain and fear by growing numbers of people. Government inefficiency, waste, corruption, and arrogance are all cited, and often with good reason.

From a biblical point of view there is great reason to suspect and scrutinize concentrations of power—not just politically but theologically. Human nature being what it is, the biblical prophets constantly warned against such concentrations of power and were especially hard on "the king," who embodied political power in biblical times. The powerful are always a threat to the powerless, according to the Bible. And the king and his court chaplains were always coming under the judgment of God, as spoken by the biblical prophets, whose concern was the common good and the plight of the poor and oppressed in particular.

Power is not bad, in and of itself, but it must always be held accountable. The Christian writer C. S. Lewis used to say that he supported democracy not because people were so naturally good but because they usually were not! Hence, decentralized political power with multiple levels of accountability and many "countervailing institutions" is theologically preferable to large, centralized, and unaccountable political structures.

Fair enough. But one should get theologically nervous in Washington when the same people who perpetually cry out against big government are silent about big business and its domination of the political process. What about the intense and growing concentration of power in the market economy? When our biggest corporations are larger and more powerful than many national governments, when big industry lobby groups literally draft legislation, isn't it fair to question their influence in the corridors of Congress?

The Democrats may indeed be too protective of the big government bureaucracies that provide much of their support, but the Republicans refuse to challenge the entrenched economic elites who are their patrons. This is the great conservative double standard. The federal welfare payments—in the form of corporate subsidies and tax breaks—that are quietly given out each year to the rich and powerful far outstrip the amounts given to the poor. Yet it is the resources given to the latter that are now the subject of controversy in the nation's capital. If we are seriously trying to reduce the deficit, why is corporate welfare to CEOs and their lawyers not on the chopping block along with the funds to poor single mothers and fatherless children?

The reasons are directly connected with the fact that welfare moms have little left over from their checks to make campaign contributions to those running for public office. If the families of the urban underclass had the clout possessed by corporate PACs representing wealthy interests, does anyone really believe that corporate welfare would stay hidden from view while the public spotlight burns down on our poorest citizens?

The biblical tradition says that the poor *should* have as much clout as those with money and power. If we take the Bible seriously, the growing gap between the haves and the have-nots in America is a massive moral and political issue. The grossly inequitable distribution of the nation's resources, the steady decline of the middle class, the dramatic increases in wealth to the upper echelons of American society, and the swelling numbers of the nation's poor are issues critical to our political health and well-being—to our civility. Yet they are almost never central topics of our public discourse.

The people who bankroll American politics don't want these topics to come up. Or as one commentator recently put it, the political silence about the growing economic divisions in American life is a "purchased silence." Whenever the topic threatens to emerge, some conservative politician will always accuse the critics of wealth of engaging in "class warfare." But the real war is that declared on both the poor and the middle class by the changing character of the global economy. The "casino economy" of Wall Street is destroying the real economy. The endless corporate mergers and relocations concentrate power in fewer and fewer hands and "downsize" both opportunity and democracy for the rest of us.

To attack big government and blame only the welfare state for the problem of poverty, while virtually ignoring the enormous power of big corporations over the political process and the dislocation and insecurity of ordinary people, is inconsistent, dishonest, and theologically untenable. If the dysfunctions of the welfare system can be scrutinized, why not the changing structure of a global economy that continues to remove jobs from American communities? If the economic system is producing greater and greater inequality, how can that not affect the quality of our political democracy? And if the government bureaucrats are going to be challenged to open up the political process, why not challenge the lobbyists for every corporate and partisan PAC, who now virtually write the laws for the same members of Congress whom their contributions put into office?

The biblical writers spoke often about the king, but they spoke just as often about the landlord, the employer, the judge, the owners of land and property, and those who live in luxury while others endure the heat of oppression. Let's remember that *oppression* is a biblical word, used by Amos, Isaiah, and Jeremiah long before the Bolshevik revolution of 1917, and it is clearly meant to describe the injustice of structures and institutions. Both political and economic institutions come under prophetic interrogation by the prophets of the Bible. It's time they came under our interrogation too.

This is not just about the need for campaign finance reform, as important as that is. It is a question of values and, indeed, the civility of the political process.

What we are calling for is nothing less than what historian Vincent Harding has called "the spiritual renewal of democracy." How do we make our democracy more real than imagined? How might political candidates and ideas be made more accountable to the whole public and not just to the elites? How might many healthy popular movements already under way help to renew the very idea of citizenship?

Opening Up the Process

Unfortunately, new political solutions, leaders, and candidates find it very hard to emerge in a tightly closed political system—a winner-take-all electoral process financed by the people and institutions who are already in control. Both new ideas and new leaders are kept outside the process by the very nature of its political and financial structure. Many of the people whose ideas we most need are the kind of community and constituency leaders who have demonstrated both a vision and a following, but do not have access to the kind of resources that could make them serious political candidates. In a political system dominated by lawyers, businessmen, and public relations experts, we need the infusion of teachers, farmers, community organizers, church elders, shop stewards, poets, young people, and PTA parents. But most of them don't have the necessary money or connections to play a part.

Recently, I was having dinner with a young Christian lawyer and his wife in Australia. Tim had served for a while as the mayor of a small inner-city community that is part of the city of Melbourne. Now working as a pastor again for a large downtown church, he has responsibilities for articulating the moral dimensions of many public issues as they impact the lives of people in that city.

Because of his success as a mayor and a pastor, and his high profile on a number of political issues, Tim was approached about a possible run for the parliament of Australia. He's been asked before and, with his wife, Meredie, declined for family reasons, including the need of young children for their father's presence. Now the questions are coming up again, and I was privileged to be included in the family discussion.

The issues being discussed were all the right ones—impact on the family, personal motivations, the temptations of political power, and whether a "prophetic" role from a church base or a "political" role in the legislature is the more effective or faithful role for Tim.

The issue of money came up only briefly and tangentially. Tim explained that all candidates receive a reimbursement of thirty cents for every vote they get, and he was assured to get enough support to cover his campaign expenses even if he lost. He also predicted the cost of his election campaign to be only in the tens of thousands of dollars.

When I told Tim and Meredie what a comparable campaign now costs in the United States (often now in seven and eight figures), they were both incredulous.

"We could never raise that kind of money," Tim exclaimed, "unless we could get the support of the very rich and powerful." Exactly.

While campaign finance reform is a critical issue in most democracies around the world today, nowhere is the situation so extreme as in the United States. In no other country do electoral campaigns cost so much money and a small, wealthy elite exert such influence and power over who runs and who wins. While the "wealth primary" is still quite hidden in American politics, its control over the political process is unquestionable.

The dominant influence of wealth and power not only limits who runs and who wins, it also serves to exclude all but a narrow range of political options and visions. In an environment so controlled by the top of the society, new political directions—especially those generated from grassroots communities—have little chance of being heard or tried on a national level.

Not surprisingly, both the Republican and Democratic parties have resisted serious efforts at campaign finance reform. Both have too much vested interest in the existing system—and both have become trapped by it. Large donors and political action committees (PACs) virtually control the political landscape and conversation because they control the two major political parties. As E. J. Dionne commented on the lack of alternative political vision in American politics today, "It's not so much that we need a third political party, but a second one."

Communities Take Charge

While the politicians of the Left and Right argue over who is most to blame, our kids are being shot in the streets. Isn't it time to call a cease-fire in our culture wars—for the sake of the children?

The 1994 elections altered the political landscape, and it was a sea change. Voters expressed a lack of confidence in a federal government that has grown over many decades and yet seems helpless to solve an interconnected series of intractable social problems that appear to be growing out of control.

Like the end of the Cold War the 1994 political discussion was pivotal. There are new opportunities in this move away from distant bureaucracies in Washington, and the answers can be found a lot closer to home—in our local communities. Community-based solutions can provide new hope where both traditional liberal and conservative solutions have failed.

I got my own start in politics when I became involved in the civil rights movement as a teenager. The social conscience that grew out of that freedom struggle infused the American spirit with a new sense of political morality. But the liberal conscience has atrophied, losing its moral foundations and political imagination. Instead it has become identified with huge, distant, and impersonal bureaucracies too often concerned more with control than caring, entrapping the poor instead of empowering them.

New hope can be found in community-based political and economic solutions that really address the root causes of urban disintegration, suburban isolation, and rural decline. In many local communities diverse people and groups are beginning to come together, seeking a politics with spiritual values that transcends the old options of Left and Right.

For example, in Boston churches have formed a Ten-Point Coalition that focuses on rebuilding both fractured families *and* shattered neighborhoods. After the killing of a six-year-old child in Chicago's Cabrini Green housing project, mothers forged a gang truce by confronting drug dealers with their personal responsibilities. In Santa Cruz, California, Barrios Unidos organizers are combining spirituality and community-based economic development—from T-shirts to computers—to end the violence in Latino neighborhoods around the nation. In Kansas City courageous pastors inspire young former gang warriors to become street organizers, who now wage peace between urban combatants.

In rural Maine land trusts and housing cooperatives offer the beginnings of an American land-reform movement. In a suburban Texas community a local town meeting makes the spiritual connections between societal violence and the materialistic values that separate us from one another and poison the hearts of both our poor and our affluent children. In Seattle the mayor plans a "retreat" for local government leaders eager to explore new political options.

In many places new partnerships between both private and public institutions seek to create jobs, revitalize schools, and hold the criminal justice system accountable. In particular, community-based economic development is showing the capacity to bring together people from across the political spectrum who share a populist preference for empowerment over either liberal policies of social control or conservative policies of social abandonment.

Finding Common Ground

But how do we address the broad moral and religious issues that plague us as a society? At a recent gathering of diverse church leaders, there was a strong consensus on issues such as the biblical priority of the poor, the theological imperative of caring for the environment, and the spiritual urgency of confronting racism in America. Less clear was how to address divisive questions such as abortion and how gay and lesbian people figure in family issues. These of course are the touchstone issues for the Religious Right and have become polarizing flash-points in the political debate. It is clear that we need new ways to address these familiar and important issues.

We cannot avoid them or simply take a libertarian stance, as candidates on both sides of the political spectrum have done. One and a half million abortions every year *is* a moral issue, as is the urgent need to rebuild our disintegrating family systems. Teenage pregnancy, family breakups, and the lack of personal responsibility are key reasons for poverty and human misery as much as are the loss of jobs, the decline of wages, the marginalization of the poor, and continuing racial injustice. Both the Left and the Right continue to make false choices about these issues of cultural breakdown and social injustice. They must be put back together.

Why can't we be committed to public policies that discourage abortion and actively seek alternatives to taking unborn lives? The crisis that many women find themselves in must be acknowledged, male irresponsibility in creating and then abandoning children must be confronted, and the society's responsibility for protecting children must be affirmed.

Why can't we create a common ground where pro-life and pro-choice people can work together to *dramatically reduce* the number of abortions in this country? That can be accomplished through providing abortion alternatives to pregnant women in crisis, offering personal and financial support to women about to make a desperate choice, combating teenage pregnancy, taking a tough stance on sexual abuse of younger women by older men, reforming the adoption process, and endorsing an agenda of justice for women on issues across the board in our society.

Actually trying to save lives could be an attractive alternative to endlessly debating a constitutional ban on abortions, which even many conservative pro-life leaders now say wouldn't really be "pro-life" if it pushes too many women into the back alleys again.

Many people would support reasonable and appropriate legal restrictions on abortion (as in most of Western Europe), but would not favor a policy that would totally criminalize abortions in this present climate. Instead, some are suggesting an approach of "cultural persuasion" to change the moral climate of our society and the political framework of the debate. The goal should be the creation of an environment where both women and children are valued and respected, and where men are held responsible for their behavior toward both. In such an environment, abortion would become "rare" and ultimately less "thinkable."

Similarly, why can't we agree that traditional two-parent families must be strengthened and supported, even by public policy, but do it in a way that doesn't scapegoat or discriminate against gay and lesbian people? The hate, fear, and violence against homosexuals, homophobia, is intolerable in a decent society and diminishes us as a nation. In a pluralistic society the rights of all citizens, including gays and lesbians, must be upheld and protected without regard to honest disagreements among people about legitimate religious and moral concerns. At the same time, we must recognize that a critical mass of healthy families with male and female role models *is* crucial for the well-being and stability of any society.

And why do we persist in the false choice between either personal responsibility or economic justice to alleviate poverty, as the conservatives and liberals continue to do? Why are we forced to favor either big government programs or the withdrawal of government altogether in the welfare debate? Poverty is created by both bad habits and the lack of economic opportunity, often in tandem. New partnerships between nonprofit organizations and governments on all levels are most likely to create the kind of "civil society" through which many of our problems can be solved.

We must not simply abandon affirmative action remedies with no alternative strategies in place for dealing with the continuing legacy of racism. Instead we can— and must—retool and update strategies to expand opportunity and fairness in our increasingly pluralistic society as we search for unity among diverse people.

We must not simply react to violence with more police, prisons, and capital punishment. Instead we can— and must—rebuild the social and moral infrastructures that we know reduce crime and support the new ventures in criminal justice arrangements that have proven to decrease recidivism.

On these and other questions we need new thinking. At the heart of any new approach will be a new political morality, a new spiritual politics. The task of forging that new politics will take us far beyond the election of 1996.

Indeed, what is most needed now is a new, and very old, "politics of vision." Beyond the politics of blame now routinely practiced by both the Left and the Right lies the possibility of some new common ground. This is the future that could bring us together. History teaches that we will only find common ground by moving to higher ground. Reaching that new ground must become our most important political task. And it will be the moral test of political leadership in the period just ahead.

Such a new politics of vision will not engage in endless and divisive recrimination, but could infuse the political process with a new sense of hope. As the "Cry for Renewal" statement said, "True biblical faith focuses on the moral values that must be recovered to heal the torn political fabric; ideological faith would rend the fabric further in the pursuit of power. Biblical faith tries to find common ground between warring factions by taking the public discourse to higher ground; ideological faith fuels the rhetoric of "us and them" and breeds a climate for hate and even violence. Biblical faith holds up the virtues of compassion and community; ideological faith appeals to personal and group self-interest. Biblical faith understands our identity as the children of God as a call to humility and reconciliation rather than the basis for attacking those who are less righteous."

Who will articulate a political vision that seeks common ground among diverse people with legitimate concerns? The politics of division will only take us lower and lower. We need a politics of values and vision today, one that takes seriously both personal and social transformation. Despite public cynicism a deep longing exists in the land for rediscovering the moral heart of our public debate.

The religious community could help lead that discussion toward new political alternatives. With that end in view we need a new dialogue embracing all sectors of the religious community, including the Religious Right. They have important concerns and deserve to be heard. But the issues of political morality are too important to be left only to one voice.

Conclusion

When we heard the weather report predicting another snowstorm on its way to Washington, D.C., our hearts sank. The Call to Renewal organizing conference was about to begin in the nation's capital and those planning it worried that people slated to attend from around the country might be dissuaded by the forecast. But on a snowy Friday morning in early February 1996, the large meeting room at the Capitol Hill Holiday Inn quickly filled up, and smiles returned to the organizers' faces. This first national gathering of the Call was announced as a "working conference," a time to train, organize, and mobilize for the election year and beyond.

Our purpose was twofold: to lift up a visible alternative to the Religious Right and to help lay the foundations for a "new politics" in America—rooted in spiritual values and beyond the old categories of both the Right and Left.

Those who gathered on that winter weekend were not there to endorse candidates or run for office. Theirs was not a partisan purpose. Rather they wanted to im-

prove the quality of our public debate and broaden the
scope of "moral discourse" beyond the narrow "litmus
tests" of the Religious Right. While affirming the crucial
importance of issues like personal responsibility, the sacredness of human life, and "family values," they
wanted to hold all those running for office accountable
to other deeply rooted religious concerns—such as the
priority of the poor, the care of the creation, and the
healing of our racial divides.

More than 250 key grassroots leaders from every region of the United States braved the snow and came
ready to work. They included evangelical pastors and
the founders of successful urban programs, Catholic social action directors and college professors engaged in
social service ministries, Pentecostal preachers from the
streets and the heads of mainline Protestant denominations, black Baptists and the leader of a movement for
Jewish renewal, students and senior citizens, community
organizers and evangelists, environmental activists and
pro-family advocates, racial justice trainers and women
priests, journalists and fund-raisers.

People came from every walk of life, eager to lift up a
public voice different from the Christian Coalition's, to
connect with others who shared their concerns, and to
mobilize for a new political vision in this country far
beyond the election year. A "network of networks" was
coming together.

The organizers who met in Washington regularly

work with people from many different traditions and constituencies around the country. They also have a much deeper agenda than just being an alternative to the Religious Right. It is the possibility of a "new politics" that most fires their spirits. On that score they connect with millions of people in this nation who are also hungry for a more "spiritual politics." Despite the attention during an election year to national politics, it will likely be the local arena where a new politics first emerges and, in fact, it already has.

A few weeks later I was in San Antonio, Texas, and was heartened to see the success of community efforts to reduce youth violence, since a rally we had held there just two years before. I vividly remember the community breakfast the morning after our rally, as pastors and community workers painfully described drive-by shootings and an atmosphere of terror on the streets. We spoke that day of the need to create "a new table" to which diverse people and groups in the community would be invited.

Two years later now, a local Lutheran pastor, who was one of the spearheads of a San Antonio antiviolence movement, picked me up at the airport. She enthusiastically reported the dramatic decrease in violence and drive-by shootings, and at least five gang peace truces made in the city. An "Antiviolence Collaborative" now involved people and groups from all around San Antonio—churches, synagogues, neighborhood organizations, community groups, businesses, the city government, police, and, most importantly, the young people themselves. She kept referring to the image they continually used of the "banquet table" to which everyone is welcome. Getting people to the table was the most important thing, and it was working there in Texas.

The image of the "table" is a powerful one for me. It runs through biblical history and it is as contemporary as the evening meal that helps hold a family together, the potluck supper that cements social and spiritual connections, or the special gathering of loved ones that marks a reunion or holiday celebration. It is at the table that we see each other's faces, remind ourselves of the ties that bind us, and rededicate ourselves to who and what we were meant to be. It is also an opportunity to be thankful for what we have so that it might not slip away.

New political visions will be born at such tables. Only by coming together can we see the possibilities that could begin to move us forward. Anyone can come to the table. If there are not enough chairs, we must find some more. If there is not enough room, we must make the table larger. Even the shape of the table will change as we discover that round tables allow us to see each other better, and on more equal terms, than the old rectangular styles.

You can find a place at the table too. Find the people in your own community who share a kindred spirit.

Connect to a group that is doing things that you believe are important. Support them with your financial contributions. Volunteer your time and energy in the inner city: mentor a child, offer your skills, share your experience, and give someone your love.

Get informed on the issues most critical to you and your community. Write letters to the editor and to your elected officials. Participate in the citizen alerts of the public policy groups you support. Get involved with direct action in your local community and, sometimes, come to Washington. Marches and demonstrations are good for the soul. Help support or even sponsor local town-meetings again, on vital topics of community concern—an election year is a good time, but so is any time. If old voices don't speak for you, help to create new ones. Perhaps you want to link up with a network like the Call to Renewal to help make those connections (see page 200).

New politics depends upon all of us. And it is more likely to trickle up than trickle down. Trickles will turn into streams, and streams into mighty rivers with the power to reshape the political landscape. Today our waters are troubled, but the future belongs to those who look, hope, pray for, and believe the promise of the prophet Amos: "Let justice roll down like waters, and righteousness like an ever-flowing stream."

APPENDIX A

Call to Renewal
Christians for a New Political Vision

"Our times call out for renewed political vision. And vision depends on spiritual values. . . . Our commitment is to diligently apply spiritual values to the questions of our public life and to offer a Christian alternative to ideological religion."

Both conservative and liberal religion in our country have too often become captive to old choices. The aggressive role the Christian Coalition has taken in the Republican party, and its claim to be a "permanent fixture on the American political landscape for people of faith," has left many searching for an alternative. The continuing identification of religious liberalism with political liberalism and the Democratic party has often lacked moral imagination or prophetic integrity.

In May 1995, more than 100 religious leaders from diverse traditions joined in "The Cry for Renewal" (reprinted below), sending a message to the nation's media and political leaders that there was an alternative Christian voice.

The statement declared, "We refuse the false choices between personal responsibility or social justice, between good values or good jobs, between strong families or strong neighborhoods, between sexual morality or civil rights for homosexuals, between the sacredness of life or the rights of women, between fighting cultural corrosion or battling racism."

This call was initiated by evangelicals, who were joined by Catholics, African-American church leaders, and mainline Protestants. It proposed that:

– there is a Christian alternative that transcends old categories of Right and Left, liberal and conservative;

– there is the necessity and possibility of a new politics—community-based, values-centered, and solution-oriented, beyond the old polarities;

– there is a new network of spiritual and social concern emerging across the spectrum of churches;

– the Christian community must refuse false choices by diligently applying the values of faith to each social and political issue.

The "Cry for Renewal" statement has now become a network—the Call to Renewal: Christians for a New Political Vision. The vision will be expressed as an alternative public voice, through a "network of networks"—uniting concerned individuals, organizations, and churches. We are not a political party or organization, but a movement affirming the vital link between spiritual renewal and social transformation.

We are working to:

– lift up a clear, visible, and credible alternative voice to the Religious Right and Left;

– organize local, city, and statewide Call to Renewal networks;

– nurture and link church-based grassroots initiatives and other ministries around the country that combine spiritual renewal and social justice;

– develop and serve a new Christian student movement that challenges students to a deeper understanding of the social implications of their faith;

– produce and distribute study curricula, biblically based voter education materials, and policy positions that express an alternative vision of faith and politics;

– assist in organizing regional conferences, candidate forums, and town meetings.

While the Call to Renewal responds to the need for a "Christian" alternative to the Christian-dominated Religious Right, the quest for a more spiritual politics is not limited to Christian or even religious people. Call to Renewal and *Sojourners* magazine (see Appendix B) also connect to other faith traditions and those whose moral conscience calls them to a new politics.

We invite you to join us. We have available a basic information packet which includes the "Cry for Renewal" statement, our action plan, a newsletter, and other educational and organizing resources.

"Let a new dialogue begin at the national, regional, and local levels around the country. Let politicized religion be replaced with prophetic faith to forge new coalitions of conscience across the land."

You can contact the Call to Renewal at:

2401 Fifteenth Street, NW
Washington, DC 20009
phone: 202/328-8842
fax: 202/328-8757
email: Call__to__Renewal@convene.com

The Cry for Renewal
Let Other Voices Be Heard

Our times cry out for renewed political vision. And vision depends upon spiritual values. We believe that the language of morality and faith can make a critical contribution to political discourse. The crisis we face is a spiritual crisis and must be responded to by solutions that address the "spirit" of the times that often lies beneath our political and economic problems. We believe further that the old political language and solutions of Right and Left, liberal and conservative are almost completely dysfunctional now and helpless to lead us into a different future. But if politics will be renewed more by moral values than by partisan warfare, the religious community must play a more positive role.

Christian faith must not become another casualty of the culture wars. Indeed, religious communities should be the ones calling for a cease-fire. The ideological polarization of the churches will not contribute to the spiritual discernment of politics the country most needs. Inflamed rhetoric and name calling is no substitute for real and prayerful dialogue between different constituencies with legitimate concerns and a gospel of love which can bring people together.

We are Evangelical voices who seek a biblical approach to politics, not an ideological agenda. We are Catholic voices who assert our own church's social teachings as a vital alternative to both the Left and the Right. We are Orthodox voices who have long stressed the role of spirituality in nurturing culture. We are African-American, Latino, white, Asian, and Native American church voices whose commitment to personal faith and social justice leads us to visions of transformation beyond both political parties. We are voices from all the Protestant churches who feel represented neither by old religious liberalism nor new right fundamentalism.

Together, we proclaim an evangelical, biblical, orthodox, and catholic faith that must address a nation in crisis. We believe that our impoverished political process needs the moral direction and energy that spiritual and religious values can contribute to the public debate. Separation of church and state rightly prevents the official establishment of any religion, but does not and must not prohibit the positive influence of religious communities on the nation's moral and political climate.

Faith and Ideology

The question is not whether religious faith should make a political contribution, but how. If religious values are to influence the public square, as we believe they should, they ought to make our political discourse more honest, moral, civil, and spiritually sensitive, especially to those without the voice and power to be fairly represented.

Recently, the increased influence of religion in politics has too often made our political debate even more divisive, polarized, and less sensitive to the poor and dispossessed.

At stake is not just politics, but the meaning of faith itself. We challenge any political litmus test that distorts the independent moral conscience that faith can bring to politics. We are dismayed by those who would undermine the integrity of religious conviction that does not conform to a narrow ideological agenda. And we are deeply concerned about the subversion of prophetic religion when wealth and power are extolled rather than held accountable, and when the gospel message is turned upside down to bring more comfort to those on the top of society than to those at the bottom.

True biblical faith focuses on the moral values that must be recovered to heal the torn political fabric; ideological faith would rend the fabric further in the pursuit of power. Biblical faith tries to find common ground between warring factions by taking the public discourse to higher ground; ideological faith fuels the rhetoric of "us and them" and breeds a climate for hate and even violence. Biblical faith holds up the virtues of compassion and community; ideological faith appeals to personal and group self-interest. Biblical faith understands our identity as the children of God as a call to humility and reconciliation rather than the basis for attacking those who are less righteous.

Old Options, False Choices, New Directions

Conformity to the old options offered by either the Religious Right or the Religious Left will not take us forward. Both conservative and liberal religion have too often become culturally captive forces that merely cheer on the ideological camps with which they are now identified. But religion as a political cheerleader is inevitably false as religion.

The almost total identification of the Religious Right with the new Republican majority in Washington is a dangerous liaison of religion with political power. With the ascendancy and influence of the Christian Right in party circles, the religious critique of power has been replaced with the religious competition for power.

Likewise, the continuing close identification of religious liberalism with political liberalism and the Democratic party has demonstrated a public witness often lacking in moral imagination or prophetic integrity. Liberal religious leaders have sought access and influence with those in power no less than their Religious Right counterparts. Neither right-wing religious nationalism nor left-wing religious lobbying will serve us at this critical historical juncture. Such faith is often more ideological than truly evangelical.

Today, the body politic is buffeted by polarized extremes. Instead of helping a politically war weary public find common concerns and values, the religious community, on both sides, has often given sanction to the perpetuation of tragic divisions.

We refuse the false choices between personal responsibility or social justice, between good values or good jobs, between strong families or strong neighborhoods, between sexual morality or civil rights for homosexuals, between the sacredness of life or the rights of women, between fighting cultural corrosion or battling racism. We call ourselves and our churches back to a biblical focus that transcends the Left and the Right. We call the Christian community to consider carefully each social and political issue, diligently apply the values of faith, and be willing to break out of traditional political categories. By seeking the biblical virtues of justice and righteousness, the Christian community could help a cynical public find new political ground.

We believe the American people are disgusted with politics as usual and hungry for political vision with spiritual values that transcends the old and failed categories that still imprison public discourse and stifle our creativity. The religious community should help lead that discussion and action toward new political and economic alternatives. We commit ourselves to that task and to dialogue with all sectors of the religious community toward that end.

"The Least of These"

We are especially concerned with the harsh rhetoric toward the powerless coming from the nation's capital. It is indeed time to re-examine old solutions that control the poor instead of empowering them. We will join with anyone in the search for new solutions rooted in local communities, moral values, and social responsibility. Many of our congregations and communities are already taking a leadership role in that task. But those Jesus told us to remember especially as "the least of these" must be neither forgotten nor scapegoated. To abandon or blame the poor for their oppression and affirm the affluent in their complacency would be a moral and religious failure, and is no alternative to social policies which have not succeeded.

Spiritual Politics

We would speak another word and offer clear criteria by which to judge morally our nation's political policies.

We serve a God who upholds the dignity and hope of the poor and a Savior who loved the little children. We must save all our children and not punish those who are disadvantaged.

We follow the One who called us to be peacemakers and gave His life to reconcile a broken humanity. We must stop the violence that has overtaken the nation, and address its root causes in the distorted spiritual values and unjust social structures in which we are all complicit.

We have a faith that invites us to conversion. We must revive the lapsed virtues of personal responsibility and character, and repent for our social sins of racism, sexism, and poverty.

We love a Creator who calls for justice and stewardship. We must begin to judge our economic and environmental habits and policies by their impact on the next generation, rather than just our own.

We are compelled to a lifestyle of service and compassion. We must seek healing from the materialism which has made us less caring and more selfish creatures, isolated us from one another, enshrined the power of money over our political processes, wounded our natural world, and poisoned the hearts of our children—rich and poor alike.

We are led by our faith into community. We must rejuvenate the moral values and political will to rebuild

our disintegrating family systems, our shattered neighborhoods, and our divided nation.

Spiritual Renewal

Politics cannot solve all our problems. Spiritual renewal
will be required—of our personal values and communal
virtues, of our religious congregations and neighborhood organizations, of our educational institutions and
economic enterprises. But genuine spiritual renewal
must not be self-righteous or mean-spirited. And spiritual sensitivity must replace ideological predictability as
the touchstone of religion in politics.

Our definitions of politics must be widened to include
new solutions and leadership. In particular, new community-based and value-centered solutions must be
found to our seemingly intractable problems. The wall
between "public" and "private" solutions must come
down in favor of new partnerships and configurations
that involve everyone. And our religious communities
must become meeting places and experimentation
grounds where those new solutions are shaped and carried out in partnership with other cultural, economic,
and political institutions.

New Voices

The issues of political morality we now confront are too important to be left to only one voice. We testify that there are other visions of faith and politics in the land. New voices are critically needed. We especially appeal to the media to let new voices now be heard. We appeal to the politicians to listen to the voices of religion rather than seeking to manipulate them.

Our commitment is to diligently apply spiritual values to the vexing questions of our public life and, where necessary, to offer a Christian alternative to ideological religion. Let a new dialogue begin at national, regional, and local levels around the country. Let politicized religion be replaced with prophetic faith to forge new coalitions of Christian conscience across the land.

Initiating Endorsers of "The Cry for Renewal"
May 23, 1995

JOHN HURST ADAMS, senior bishop, African Methodist Episcopal Church

LOUISE AKERS SC, Leadership Conference of Women Religious

MYRON AUGSBURGER, president emeritus, Christian College Coalition

NATHAN O. BAXTER, dean, Washington National Cathedral

DAVID BECKMAN, president, Bread for the World

SCOTT W. BOLINDER, Zondervan Publishing House

MANFRED BRAUCH, president, Eastern Baptist Theological Seminary

VERY REV. GERALD L. BROWN SS, president, Catholic Conference of Major Superiors of Men's Institutes

RT. REV. EDMOND L. BROWNING, presiding bishop, Episcopal Church

CALVIN O. BUTTS III, Abyssinian Baptist Church

MARGARET CAFFERTY PBVM, executive director, Leadership Conference of Women Religious

JOAN BROWN CAMPBELL, general secretary, National Council of Churches

TONY CAMPOLO, evangelical author and preacher

DANIEL R. CHAMBERLAIN, president, Houghton College

JOAN CHITTISTER, past president, Leadership Conference of Women Religious

HARVIE CONN, Westminster Theological Seminary

GORDON COSBY, Church of the Saviour

JAMES H. COSTEN, Interdenominational Theological Center

CAROL CROSSED, Seamless Garment Network

LYN CRYDERMAN, Zondervan Publishing House

ELLSWORTH CULVER, Mercy Corps International

YVONNE DELK, Community Renewal Society

MARIE DENNIS, Maryknoll Justice and Peace

REV. LARRY E. DIXON, African Methodist Episcopal Church

REV. LESLIE DOWDELL, Community Renewal Society

JAMES DUNN, Baptist Joint Committee

WILLIAM DYRNESS, Fuller Theological Seminary

MARIAN WRIGHT EDELMAN, founder and president, Children's Defense Fund

REV. DR. MILTON B. EFTHIMIOU, ecumenical officer, Greek Orthodox Archdiocese of N. and S. America

TED ENGSTROM, president emeritus, World Vision

REV. DONALD FAIRLEY, Avalon Park United Church of Christ

DAVID FISHER, pastor, Park Street Church, Boston

DR. JAMES FORBES, Riverside Church

RICHARD FOSTER, president, Renovare

MILLARD FULLER, president, Habitat for Humanity

WAYNE C. GORDON, Lawndale Community Church

WES GRANBERG-MICHAELSON, general secretary, Reformed Church in America

BISHOP DR. C. MILTON GRANHUM, New Covenant Church of Philadelphia

FRED GREGORY, president, World Concern

BISHOP THOMAS J. GUMBLETON, Catholic Archdiocese of Detroit

REV. DR. RICHARD HAMM, general minister and president, Christian Church/Disciples of Christ

PETE HAMMOND, InterVarsity Christian Fellowship

REV. RAY HAMMOND, Ten-Point Coalition

STEVE HAYNER, InterVarsity Christian Fellowship

J. BRYAN HEHIR, Harvard Center for International Affairs

WILL L. HERZFELD, Evangelical Lutheran Church in America

ROBERTA HESTENES, president, Eastern College

LUTHER HOLLAND JR., Chicago Metropolitan Association, United Church of Christ

GRETCHEN HULL, Christians for Biblical Equality

TED KEATING, Conference of Major Superiors of Men's Institutes

FR. LEONID KISHKOVSKY, Ecumenical Officer, Orthodox Church

REV. ARCHIE LeMONE, Progressive National Baptist Convention, Inc.

BISHOP RAYMOND A. LUCKER, Catholic Diocese of New Ulm, Minnesota

REV. TIMOTHY McDONALD, Iconium Baptist Church

BISHOP GEORGE D. McKINNEY, pastor, St. Stephen's Church of God in Christ

LOIS McKINNEY, Trinity Evangelical Divinity School

GORDON MACDONALD, pastor, Grace Chapel

LUIS MADRIGAL, Hispanic Association of Bilingual Bicultural Ministries

KAREN MAINS and DAVID MAINS, Chapel of the Air Ministries

REV. MICHAEL A. MATA, Urban Leadership Institute, Claremont School of Theology

BISHOP LEROY T. MATTHIESEN, Catholic Diocese of Amarillo, Texas

JOHAN MAURER, Friends United Meeting

KEN MEDEMA, pastor and musician

REV. DR. DONALD E. MILLER, Church of the Brethren

CALVIN MORRIS, vice-president, Interdenominational Theological Center

BISHOP P. FRANCIS MURPHY, Catholic Archdiocese of Baltimore

REV. DR. REAVES F. NAHWOOKS, Lincoln and Omaha Indian Community Churches

REV. DR. SUSAN D. NEWMAN, pastor, First Congregational Church, United Church of Christ

DAN O'NEILL, president, Mercy Corp. International

J. I. PACKER, theologian

WILLIAM PANNELL, Fuller Theological Seminary

JOHN PERKINS, Christian Community Development Association

SPENCER PERKINS, Urban Family

REV. GREGORY REISERT OFM Cap., executive director, Catholic Conference of Major Superiors of Men's Institutes

REV. EUGENE RIVERS, Ten-Point Coalition

RICHARD ROHR OFM, author

BISHOP PETER A. ROSAZZA, Catholic Archdiocese of Hartford, Connecticut

BRUCE RYSKAMP, Zondervan Publishing House

REV. DR. PAUL SHERRY, president, United Church of Christ

RON SIDER, president, Evangelicals for Social Action

TOM SINE, author and lecturer

J. ALFRED SMITH, Allen Temple Baptist Church

HOWARD SNYDER, United Theological Seminary

REV. DR. GORDON SOMMERS, Moravian Church in America

BISHOP WALTER F. SULLIVAN, Catholic Diocese of Richmond, Virginia

BISHOP MELVIN G. TALBERT, United Methodist Church

HAROLD DEAN TRULEAR, New York Theological Seminary

SR. CARLOTTA ULLMER, Sisters of St. Francis of the Holy Cross

ELDIN VILLAFANE, professor, Gordon Conwell Theological Seminary

JIM WALLIS, Sojourners

ARCHBISHOP REMBERT G. WEAKLAND, Catholic
  Archdiocese of Milwaukee
DAN WEISS, American Baptist Churches USA
REV. DR. JEREMIAH A. WRIGHT, JR., pastor, Trinity United Church of Christ

Organizations for identification purposes only.

APPENDIX B

Sojourners

In 1971, Jim Wallis and a group of other young seminary students had a dream. It was a dream of a place where concerned people who wanted to connect their commitments to social transformation and spiritual renewal could gather. It was a dream of a place where the voice of change could be heard, where steps of action could be taken, and where an alternative vision could take root and become reality.

Today that dream is called *Sojourners*. Through the publication of a bimonthly magazine, creative public action focusing on the major issues of our day, and a growing network of individuals, groups, churches, and organizations that want to work for change in their lives, the nation, and the world, Sojourners is working to change the "soul of politics."

If you have been stirred by this book and want to get involved in this transformation, we invite you to join us. The next step is to become a member of Sojourners. Simply write or call. As a member, you will receive the bimonthly magazine, featuring a column by Jim Wallis, as well as news, features, and reviews all written from the perspective of social transformation and spiritual renewal. You will also support concrete activities such as The Things that Make for Peace, a church-based, Anti-Violence Network working with urban youth, and other peace and justice efforts around the world. You will also be kept informed about the progress of the Call to Renewal, a newly formed network offering an alternative to the Religious Right and seeking a new spiritual politics beyond the old categories of Right and Left.

Sojourners
2401 15th St., NW
Washington, DC 20009
1-800-714-7474

5176